MOTHER'S HOUSE

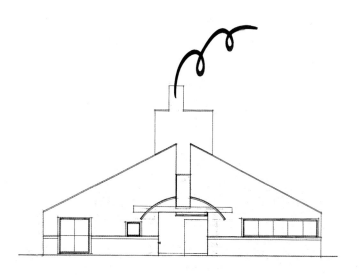

This book is dedicated to all mothers,

especially mine,

and my father, too.

PREFACE BY ALDO ROSSI WITH ESSAYS BY VINCENT SCULLY AND ROBERT VENTURI

MOTHER'S HOUSE

THE EVOLUTION OF VANNA VENTURI'S HOUSE IN CHESTNUT HILL

EDITED AND INTRODUCED BY FREDERIC SCHWARTZ

RIZZOLI
NEW YORK

First published in the United States of America in 1992
by Rizzoli International Publications, Inc.
300 Park Avenue South, New York, N.Y. 10010

Copyright © 1992 Rizzoli International Publications, Inc.

Library of Congress Cataloging-in-Publication Data
Mother's House: The Evolution of Vanna Venturi's House in Chestnut Hill /
edited by Frederic Schwartz:
with essays by Vincent Scully and Robert Venturi:
preface by Aldo Rossi.
p. cm.
ISBN 0-8478-1141-7 (hc) — ISBN 0-8478-1142-5 (pbk)
1. Vanna Venturi House (Philadelphia, Pa.)
2. Venturi, Robert—Criticism and interpretation.
3. Eclecticism in architecture—Pennsylvania—Chestnut Hill (Philadelphia)
4. Philadelphia (Pa.)—Buildings, structures, etc.
5. Chestnut Hill (Philadelphia, Pa.)—Buildings, structures, etc.
I. Schwartz, Frederic.
II. Scully, Vincent Joseph, 1920–
III. Venturi, Robert.
NA7238.P5M58 1992   92-5315
728'. 372'092—dc20   CIP

Designed and composed by *Group* **C** (BC, SAH, DK, GS, CT)
New Haven / San Francisco

Printed and bound in Hong Kong

Front cover: Vanna Venturi House, front elevation
Photo by Rollin LaFrance, courtesy of Venturi, Scott Brown and Associates

Back cover: Vanna Venturi House, back elevation
Photo by Rollin LaFrance, courtesy of Venturi, Scott Brown and Associates

PHOTO CREDITS, PAGES 95–220
Rollin LaFrance,
    courtesy of Venturi, Scott Brown and Associates
    pp. 203–211, p. 213
George Pohl,
    courtesy of Venturi, Scott Brown and Associates
    pp. 216–219
Denise Scott Brown
    p. 220
Ezra Stoller/Esto
    p. 212, pp. 214–215
Venturi, Scott Brown and Associates
    pp. 95–97, pp. 107–109, pp. 117–118, pp. 129–130,
    pp. 145–146, pp. 157–158, p. 202

THANK YOU

First and foremost, I would like to thank Robert Venturi and Denise Scott Brown for their enthusiastic support and collaboration on this and countless other projects over the past seventeen years and James Venturi for his personal insight and computer skills.

I am especially grateful to Vincent Scully for his brilliant essay and to Aldo Rossi for his poetic and timely foreword.

I acknowledge the unknowing support through their lessons of my history professors at Harvard University—Stanislaus von Moos, Eduard F. Sekler, and J. B. Jackson—and my design professors at the University of California at Berkeley—Joseph Esherick and Marc Treib.

I am grateful for the guidance, support, and especially the patience of David Morton, my editor at Rizzoli, as he has seen this book through its various stages. I especially thank Brad Collins and Diane Kasprowicz for their elegant book design.

I appreciate the cooperation of The Museum of Modern Art for the use of its model photographs, and the Deutsches Art Museum for the use of the photographs of the drawings in its collection.

I am very grateful for the cooperation of the office of Venturi, Scott Brown and Associates—Steven Estock, Matt Wargo, Jean Barker, and Linda Payne and especially Steve Izenour for his never-ending support and friendship. I am extremely indebted to my friend and client Joan Kron, who kindly gave her time and well-known editorial advice.

A special thanks to Carolina Vacarro, the Italian co-author of my first book, and my dear friend Françoise Blanc for their encouragement at the very start of this project and to Steven Newman, my best friend since our Little League days, for his support for everything I attempt.

Finally, I would like to thank Elizabeth Ward for her constant enthusiasm and editing skills. Without her, this book would still be at home in my Mac.

Frederic Schwartz New York, 1992

CHARLES H. WOODWARD
8031 GERMANTOWN AVENUE
CHESTNUT HILL
PHILADELPHIA 18, PA.
———
CHESTNUT HILL 7-5700

June 18, 1962

Mr Robert Venturi
140 North 17th Street
Philadelphia 3, Penna

Dear Mr Venturi

My brothers and I, as officers of George Woodward, Incorporated,
discussed at some length the model and plans of your proposed
house on land off Millman Street under Agreement of Sale between
George Woodward, Incorporated and yourself.   As you know, this
Agreement of Sale provides that the Woodward corporation must
approve the exterior plans of any house before settlement is made
for the ground.

My brothers are perfectly willing to approve an avant-garde house
as long as it is only controversial and not detrimental to the
neighborhood.   As you yourself mentioned, the chimney appears to
be out of proportion and worries both my brothers and myself quite
a bit.   I would be interested in seeing the model with this
chimney reduced in height.

As I told you on the telephone, my brother Stanley was quite dubious
about your exterior stairway to the second floor.   From our own
experience we know that these are apt to collect windblown papers
and become trash traps because, in many cases, they are not
thoroughly cleaned every day.   My brother Stanley was also a
little concerned about the truncated "W" forming the parapet at the
upper end of these outside stairs.

In other words, we cannot approve the plans as submitted. However,
I feel confident that, if you are still interested, you can keep the
feeling of the house and yet remove some of the controversial
elements of design.   I am somewhat reluctant to limit any architect
in attempting something new, but, unfortunately, there are too many
neighbors that will have to continually look at the house, and since
they cannot stick it in a closet like a painting, they will make
many nasty comments to us, which we do not want.

Very sincerely yours

CHW.m

CONTENTS

PREFACE

I am writing these lines out of my profound admiration for Robert Venturi, an admiration that has recently turned into a warm friendship. I preface my remarks with this comment in order to clarify the reason I am writing this essay, even if I am not writing "only" about Robert Venturi's first house. In an era inundated by anthologies, magazines, novelties, discoveries of new styles, and a babel of exhibits, it seems an excellent idea to devote a book to a single work.

Looking at the galleys of this book, I feel as though I have rediscovered an interest in architecture which I had gradually been losing. By losing I mean that every design is rooted in other sources, perhaps only in hints and memories, or in research whose objective is no longer clear to me.

But other things remain fixed: constructions, buildings, and architecture are aligned as if in a museum. I could list them as in a catalogue in no need of comment. Some buildings leap to mind as if emerging from the aftermath of a disaster and transcend time: those of Asplund, Saarinen, Berlage, and others.

In America, Louis Kahn, whose interpretation of Rome at once irritates and fascinates me, produced buildings and designs that made a strong impression on me. I find something similar in the Vanna Venturi House. Here I am speaking about this book, and the moving experience of following the young architect's design and the repeated variations that should not be taken as a sign of uncertainty. He was conscious of following a precise path with no turning back, and each variation led him to a result that had been clear from the outset.

We know that real research separates us from the crowd, and I do not believe we bother about recognition, scorn, or approval; what is going to happen will happen anyway. There is something unpredictable about great work, and I too believe that "if we sought something we not only sought that something."

Authentic research (in life as in art) leads us in a direction that initially seems secondary, but then invades our innermost being. I think of Michelangelo's followers, mannerists who pursued only one aspect of his work, perhaps the most disquieting one, and of the others who developed the most academic aspect.

Thus, for many, the Vanna Venturi House favored the most superficial aspect of so-called postmodernism, but instead it liberated architecture in America and elsewhere.

It is difficult to separate this house from the book *Learning from Las Vegas*. The authors discovered part of the American city, something that we all seemed to know but that is now clearer. This "cultivated" aspect of the architect, including writing and teaching, places him in a particular and inevitable situation; and so it is clear that the first house comes to terms with culture and creativity. I believe that culture, some form of culture, is inseparable from creativity. And so modernity is the continuation of a long journey, perhaps controversial but never interrupted.

Robert Venturi was also fortunate in the reception of his first work; and in this sense I believe that America has a capacity to understand, a kind of innocence, that old Europe does not know. I would also say that his mother's house contains a kind of innocence.

Vanna Venturi's house embodies dedication and exaltation at the same time. In subsequent work Robert Venturi and Denise Scott Brown knew how to maintain this quality, and now, I believe, they are among the best architects and teachers. This house remains something unique for all of us. Now that we have it detailed in this book, it appeals to us even more. It represents a moment in the history of architecture and society, a fixed point in time.

And this is no small accomplishment in an era that has lost its center and even the signs whereby to find it again.

Milan, 1991

FREDERIC SCHWARTZ

FOREWORD

My first contact with Robert Venturi and Denise Scott Brown was in the summer of 1975, during my first year as a graduate student at Harvard, while renovating their Art Nouveau house in the West Mount Airy section of Philadelphia. A few years earlier, my sister had given me *Complexity and Contradiction in Architecture*[1] as a high school graduation present. Some present. I tried to read it; I wasn't that smart.

One evening after work, I visited the house that Robert had designed for his mother. I had studied the house as an undergraduate at Berkeley and frankly could not figure out what all the fuss was about. It looked pretty good to me, but what was the big deal? As a student in the late sixties and early seventies, you were either for this house and the architecture it represented or against it.[2] Sides were drawn. There were two architectural schools of thought—the "whites" and the "greys."[3] The whites represented the purity of modern architecture and included architects such as Richard Meier, Peter Eisenman, and Michael Graves (he was a white then). The greys seemed to represent everything else in architecture and included Charles Moore, Robert Stern, and Venturi. I was then a student at Harvard; I had to choose—was I a white or a grey?

That first visit to the house only added to my confusion. In the twilight of evening, sitting smack in the middle of a plain green lawn, the house seemed surreal. Was it big or was it small? Was it modern or was it classical? Was it simple or complex? That summer I kept going back.

The idea for this book occurred six years later, in 1981, when I was director of the New York office of Venturi, Rauch and Scott Brown[4] and organizing an exhibition of the firm's drawings at the Max Protetch Gallery in Manhattan.[5] While searching through the archives, I found a hidden treasure for a young architect. Rolled tightly in tubes among hundreds of others were four containers of sketches, presentation and construction drawings that constitute this book. The "discovery" of these drawings was a revelation, and as time passed I became more and more interested in unearthing the roots of the design and its process.

The drawings are the complete record of the design for a small domestic masterpiece that challenged the definition of modern architecture and redefined the conception of what a house should look like. Its historical references, use of symbolism, color, and ornament were profound and provocative during a period of almost universal acceptance of orthodox modern design.

While familiar with the drawings of the house as built, I had no idea that there was a series of earlier designs, some of which appear to have little

bearing on the final design. Essentially, there were one hundred drawings of five preliminary design schemes, which follow a steady course of development, plus a final design. While the architecture of the first five schemes is brash and confident, some drawings are tentative, others unfinished, and many show a redundancy in plan, section, and elevation. They also exhibit Venturi's dilemma of reconciling his encyclopedic knowledge of historical architecture—including all the attributes he held so dear—with the high modernism of the times. He refers to both Le Corbusier [fig.1] and Frank Furness [fig.2] at the same time. The designs also suggest a lengthy struggle with Kahn (discussed in detail in Vincent Scully's essay in this book).[6] Venturi was interested in the quality of light, the layering of space, and "things wrapping around things"—concepts often attributed solely to Louis Kahn.

The final design, Scheme VI, is an abrupt departure from the progression of earlier alternatives and is a return to many of the characteristics of his Beach House project of 1959. The design in its whole and parts explores ideas that Venturi had been wrestling with since its inception. The house illustrates that architectural elements can be used

symbolically and that history includes both the distant and recent past. A single, thin, unadorned, structural steel column in the dining room—a reference to Le Corbusier—and the shiplike pipe rail of the basement stairs suggest that modern architecture is also part of the history we can learn from. Starting in the seventies, Venturi's history lesson would be taken to the extreme, with the arrival of the strict historicism of some postmodernists.[7]

3

The final version of the house also blurs the lines between popular culture and architecture. During the years Venturi designed Vanna's house, pop art came of age. Jasper Johns's *Painted Bronze*, of 1960, had been exhibited, Andy Warhol had painted his *Jackie* and *Marilyn* series in 1962, and Claes Oldenburg had exhibited his large-scale sculptures of food and household objects at a number of galleries. If a Campbell's Soup can [fig.3] was serious art, then one could wonder why a modern house couldn't look like a house, instead of a steamship or a cubist collage. The house for his mother was Venturi's own version of Jasper Johns's American flag.

In *From Bauhaus to Our House* Tom Wolfe wrote about Venturi: "It was time to

remove architecture from the elite world of the universities—from the compounds—and make it once more familiar, comfortable, cozy, and appealing to ordinary people; and to remove it from the level of theory and restore it to the compromising and inconsistent but nevertheless rich terrain of real life."[8] The seemingly simple drawings of the front elevation with its tacked-on arched opening, a big window that looked like a window, and a tall chimney within the all-encompassing outline of the pediment roof, suggest a new populist architecture—an architecture for people as well as architects. The front of the house looks almost like a house, as if a child—make that a very smart child—had drawn it [fig.4]. In Venturi's 1982 Gropius Lecture at Harvard University he stated: "Some have said my mother's house looks like a child's drawing of a house, representing the fundamental elements of shelter—gable roof, chimney, door, and windows. I like to think this is so, that it achieves another essence, that of the genre that is house and is elemental."[9]

Venturi's rise to international prominence twenty-five years ago was concurrent with the first publication on his mother's house and his book *Complexity and Contradiction in*

4

5

Architecture. Venturi recalls, "What I wrote in the book was what I was thinking about while I was drawing the house. But the design was not a conscious and direct illustration of the ideas. I was and am not that dogmatic."[10] In the quarter century since its construction, the house has become recognized worldwide; on any day busloads of architects, cameras in hand, descend on the property. The house now ranks among the most significant in the history of architecture, finding its place among others such as Villa Rotonda by Andrea Palladio [fig.5], Villa Savoye by Le Corbusier [fig.6], and Fallingwater by Frank Lloyd Wright [fig.7]. It is interesting to note that these three great architects also wrote the most important treatises on architecture.[11] Venturi joined this select group with the publication of *Complexity and Contradiction in Architecture*, which Vincent Scully has called "the most important book on the making of architecture since Le Corbusier's *Vers une Architecture* of 1923."[12] Venturi's book is still in print after twenty-five years and has been published in twelve languages.

The house would prove to be a brick thrown at the window of modernism. Steven Izenour, a student of Venturi at the University of Pennsylvania and later a co-author of *Learning from Las Vegas*,[13] remembers that other professors warned students not to go look at the building because of its ornamentation and violation of the principles of modern architecture. What serious architect would have windows with trim or paint a building green? Of course the students made a beeline to Chestnut Hill.

Despite the controversy it stirred up, Vanna's house was instantly recognized in the architectural community. It received a Gold Medal Award in 1965 from the Architectural League of New York; the selection committee included Arthur Drexler, curator of architecture and design at The Museum of Modern Art.[14] The house and its architect were selected in 1965 by Robert Stern and Philip Johnson for the Architectural League of New York's important exhibition of young American Architects—"40 under 40." Stern wrote, "Robert Venturi is now, at the critical age of forty, an acknowledged innovator. The house is, undeniably, a work of great significance."[15] In a 1966 article in *American Builder* on residential designs by the "country's outstanding young architects," the house was selected as a prototype for future models; it was one of five

6

designs for "new kinds of houses, new shapes and dimensions and new concepts."[16] In 1989 this "new kind of house" was honored as a masterpiece of American architecture with the coveted American Institute of Architects 25-Year Award.[17] It was the first house to win that award in its first year of eligibility.

In its thirty-year history, much has been written about this house. If there is one single picture associated with Robert Venturi's work and postmodern architecture, it is the front of his mother's house. Venturi's education suggested that this house should not be designed to be too original, though it is, or to make a point, though it does, but to solve real problems in ways that communicate both questions and answers. It is only now, with the passage of three decades, that certain things become clear. Its design is both straightforward and idiosyncratic, ideological and witty, and visionary and practical. It is part of history and

historically incorrect. The simplicity of its front elevation masks its intellectual complexity. These dichotomies are the essence of its power and make it one of the most celebrated images of architecture in the second half of this century.[18]

This publication includes more than one hundred previously unreleased drawings accompanied by the original description of the house.[19] The great Italian architect and theorist Aldo Rossi brings his own special sensibilities in a timely preface. A new retrospective essay by Venturi places the house in its historical context and illustrates how ideas once radical are now commonplace. (How do the Beatles sound to you today?) Vincent Scully, America's premier architectural historian, eloquently traces the design and its process through the drawings and explores Venturi's complex relationship with Louis Kahn. This, then, is the first comprehensive study of one of the most important buildings of the twentieth century.

ILLUSTRATIONS

1. Le Corbusier, Villa Savoye, Poissy, France, 1929–31, from Le Corbusier and Pierre Jeanneret, *Oeuvre Complète, 1929–34*

2. Frank Furness, University of Pennsylvania Library, Philadelphia, Pennsylvania, 1888–91, photo by Matt Wargo, courtesy of Venturi, Scott Brown and Associates

3. Andy Warhol, *Campbell's Soup*, 1965. Oil silkscreened on canvas, 36 1/8 x 24" Collection, The Museum of Modern Art, New York. Philip Johnson Fund

4. Venturi and Rauch, Vanna Venturi House, Chestnut Hill, Philadelphia, 1964, front elevation, courtesy of Venturi, Scott Brown and Associates

5. Andrea Palladio, Villa Rotunda, Vicenza, Italy, circa 1566–69, photo by Studio Tapparo & Trentin

6. Le Corbusier, Villa Savoye, Poissy, France, 1929–31, photo by Denise Scott Brown

7. Frank Lloyd Wright, Fallingwater, Bear Run, Pennsylvania, 1935, photo by Frederic Schwartz

8. Venturi and Rauch, Vanna Venturi House, Chestnut Hill, Philadelphia, Pennsylvania, 1964, front elevation, photo by Rollin LaFrance, courtesy of Venturi, Scott Brown and Associates

NOTES

1. Robert Venturi, *Complexity and Contradiction in Architecture* (New York: The Museum of Modern Art Papers on Architecture, in association with the Graham Foundation for the Advanced Studies in the Fine Arts, Chicago, 1966).

2. Some things never change. In the September 1991 issue of *Architecture*, the journal of the American Institute of Architects, a readers' poll placed Venturi in fifth place as both the most admired architect and the most disliked. He was the only architect to be selected for both lists.

3. "Five on Five," *Architectural Forum* (May 1973): 46–57. A group of articles by Robert Stern, Jaquelin Roberston, Charles Moore, Romaldo Giurgola, and Allan Greenberg offered a critical view of the work of and the book on *Five Architects* which initiated a lengthy debate between the two philosophical camps.

4. The firm has had four names since its beginning in 1960: Venturi and Short, 1960–64; Venturi and Rauch, 1964–80; Venturi, Rauch and Scott Brown, 1980–88; Venturi, Scott Brown and Associates, 1989 to the present.

5. "Buildings and Drawings," Venturi, Rauch and Scott Brown, September 15–October 16, 1982, Max Protetch Gallery, New York.

6. Venturi's relationship to Kahn, about which Venturi has spoken little, has been the subject of speculation among architectural historians and critics. Denise Scott Brown discusses Venturi and Kahn's relationship in her essay "A Worm's Eye View of Recent Architectural History," *Architectural Record* (February 1984): 69–81.

7. Charles Jencks, *The Language of Post-Modern Architecture* (New York: Rizzoli, 1977).

8. Tom Wolfe, *From Bauhaus to Our House* (New York: Farrar Straus Giroux, 1981): 104.

9. Robert Venturi, "Diversity, Relevance and Representation in Historicism, or Plus ça Change . . . plus A Plea for Pattern all over Architecture, with a Postscript on My Mother's House," The Walter Gropius Lecture, Graduate School of Design, Harvard University, April 15, 1982, *Architectural Record* (June 1982): 114–119. Venturi has stated in numerous articles, including the one in this book, that the house looks like one drawn by a child.

10. Robert Venturi, interview with the author, October 2, 1991.

11. Andrea Palladio, *Quattro Libri*, 1570; Le Corbusier, *Vers une Architecture*, 1923; Frank Lloyd Wright, *An Autobiography*, 1943.

12. Robert Venturi, *Complexity and Contradiction in Architecture*: 9.

13. Robert Venturi, Denise Scott Brown, and Steven Izenour, *Learning from Las Vegas* (Cambridge, Massachusetts: MIT Press, 1972).

14. Architectural League of New York: Architecture and Arts Awards, 1965.

15. Robert A. M. Stern, ed. *40 under 40*. Catalogue to the exhibition. (New York: Architectural League of New York, 1966): 37.

16. *American Builder* (October 1966): 60–61.

17. Michael Crosbie, "Venturi's House for his Mother Wins AIA 25-Year Award," *Architecture* (May 1989): 28.

18. "Robert Venturi has expanded and redefined the limits of the art of architecture in this century, as perhaps no other has, through his theories and built works," proclaimed the jury at the awarding of the prestigious 1991 Pritzker Prize for Architecture.

19. Heinrich Klotz first published twelve drawings of Mother's House in *Die Revision der Moderne: Postmoderne Architektur, 1960–1980*, Prestel-Verlag, Munich, 1984. These drawings are referenced by a "DAM" (Deutsches Architekturmuseum) notation in the drawing list in this book.

FREDERIC SCHWARTZ

INTRODUCTION

"And yet architecture was never old and it will ever be new." [1]

In 1959, Vanna Venturi asked her son Robert to design a house. Completed five years later in 1964, this small suburban house is unconsciously the first postmodern building and arguably the *first postmodern anything*. Revolutionary in its ideas during a period of high modernism, the design challenged and changed the course of architecture. Filled with invention and experiment, Venturi's house for his mother is perhaps the most important building of the late twentieth century, and represents the start of the brilliant career of one of the world's most influential architects.[2]

Robert Venturi's mother, Vanna, was born in Washington, D.C., in 1893. Her parents were poor immigrants from the region of Apuglia in southeastern Italy. She was a fiercely independent young woman interested in literature and liberal causes.[3] An active Socialist, she did not vote for Franklin D. Roosevelt, but for Norman Thomas the five times he ran for president. Venturi credits his mother for her "sound but unorthodox positions, socialist and pacifist, [that] worked to prepare me to feel almost all right as an outsider."[4]

Venturi's father, Robert, Sr., arrived in America in 1890 at the age of nine from the town of Atessa in the Abruzzi region, east of Rome on the Adriatic Sea. His father's father was a builder in Italy, but in America he started a fruit and produce business. When he was sixteen, Robert, Sr.'s father died and he had to quit school to take care of the family and run the store. Venturi remembers that his father had "an enormous sense of responsibility and commitment to his family." As a hard-working young man, he became a successful and well-known merchant in Philadelphia,[5] but he dreamed of becoming an architect.

Robert, Sr., and Vanna were married in 1924 and moved into a house in the suburban Philadelphia area of Upper Darby. Both were Catholic but did not practice. A year later their only child, Robert, was born, and when he was five, his parents joined the Society of Friends (Quakers) because they were pacifists and also wanted their son to have a religious affiliation.

Venturi's parents shared a common interest and love of architecture, and they filled their house with books, beautiful furniture, and objects. His mother was especially interested in furniture and fashion. (Venturi possesses an encyclopedic knowledge of furniture, and can date almost any dress since the eighteenth century within a few years.) In 1922 his father built a modest store that was designed by the well-known Philadelphia architect Edmund Brumbaugh. There is also a story that another well-known, elderly Philadelphia architect, Phineas Paiste, while a dinner guest of the family, got down on his hands and knees and built an imposing structure of blocks for the child. When it was completed, the five-year-old swept it away with one arm and said, "Now I'll show you how to do it." Venturi's loving father gently encouraged his son's interest in architecture:

I remember vividly on one of my first trips to New York City—maybe I was ten years old—my father's impulsively instructing the cab driver to pull over and wait as we approached the old Penn Station on 7th Avenue, and then conducting me down the gallery that overlooked the great hall based on the Baths of Caracalla [fig.1]. I shall never forget the breathtaking revelation of that monumental civic space bathed in ambient light from clerestories above.[6]

Robert attended the Lansdowne Friends School until he was ten years old, and he recalls, "From a very early age, I knew I wanted to be an architect; I still remember noting my favorite buildings on the bus route to grade school."[7] He later attended the more structured Episcopal Academy in Philadelphia, where he was perhaps the only Italian-American. He never attended public school because his mother, as an expression of her pacifism, did not believe in the "coercive patriotism" that forced students to recite the pledge of allegiance. (In 1943, the Supreme Court would concur.) Venturi recalls that his mother "was in a way a 'Jewish' mother. She was the dominant parent. When I look back now, I realize my father was influential on me too, but not in the direct ways she was."[8]

From 1944 to 1947 Venturi majored in architecture as an undergraduate in the Department of Art and Archaeology at Princeton University, where he had a brilliant career and graduated *summa cum laude*.[9] His architectural training began in earnest when he studied in the master's program at Princeton's Graduate School of Architecture from

1

1947 to 1950. Venturi remembers, "At Princeton I was truly a student, not a kind of seminarian receiving the word that was to be universally disseminated. At the Princeton of my time we students of architecture were encouraged to go beyond."[10] His important influences at Princeton were the noted French Beaux-Arts-trained architectural design critic Jean Labatut and the social and architectural historian Donald Drew Egbert.

Venturi was influenced by Labatut's idea of a modernism that evolved within a historical framework and solved problems without dictating a style. Venturi often speaks of Labatut's important role in his development.

Labatut brilliantly illuminated the principles of modern design to us. But modern architecture did not represent a culmination for all time, but rather a vocabulary appropriate for our time. He saw modern architecture as a beginning, not an end—but a beginning interpreted in the context of history. And history, for Labatut, was not a way to prove points, but an objective basis for enriching our vision, and an instrument, ultimately, for liberating our work. Modern architecture was not a revolutionary ideology to be instilled, but a stage in historical evolution, which, by implication, we artists, through education, could grow from.[11]

At Princeton, Venturi's closest mentor was Donald Drew Egbert. Venturi took Egbert's course in the history of modern architecture four times: "I sat in on it as a freshman, was the slide projectionist as a sophomore, took it for credit as a junior, and taught it as a graduate school teaching assistant. Egbert's history was inclusive, a complex evolution rather than a dramatic revelation, made up of social and symbolic, as well as formal and technological, imperatives. Egbert studied history to search for the truth, never to prove a point."[12] Venturi saw a place for himself in both Labatut's and Egbert's views of an evolving modernism.

In 1947, at the age of twenty-two, while working in the summer for the Philadelphia architect Robert Montgomery Brown, Venturi met Louis Kahn in an elevator. Three years later Venturi invited Kahn and the noted Philadelphia architect George Howe[13] to his thesis jury at Princeton.[14] In the summer of 1948, Venturi "walked on air" during his first, three-month-long, trip to Europe,

2

when he visited England, France, and Italy. One of the first buildings he visited, Blenheim Palace [fig.2], would later influence the design of his mother's house.

After graduation in 1950, Venturi began work in Oscar Stonorov's office in Philadelphia. He was in charge of the organization of an important exhibition of Frank Lloyd Wright's drawings and models at Gimbel Brothers department store in Philadelphia, which would later travel to Italy. Venturi recalls how thrilled he was as he handled the early sketches and drawings of Fallingwater and other buildings by Wright that arrived in great boxes from Taliesin. He revered Wright and had had the good fortune to sit next to him three years earlier at a luncheon celebrating Princeton's bicentennial, and found him both friendly and engaging.

On the recommendation of Kahn, Venturi worked for Eero Saarinen in Detroit from 1951 to 1953, enjoying the opportunities of a large, successful firm and the stimulus of a number of extraordinarily talented young architects, including Kevin Roche and Gunnar Birkerts. Venturi says, "Although I was respected and given a lot of responsibility at Saarinen's office, I saw myself in a new context where I was an outsider and did not fit in. But it was an important time when I learned a lot about myself."[15] He worked on the General Motors Technical Center in Detroit and the Milwaukee War Memorial Auditorium.

During this time, Venturi's father's health was deteriorating, and he returned home for eighteen months in 1953 to help run and reorganize the family fruit and produce business.

In 1954, on his third attempt, Venturi finally won the prestigious Rome Prize Fellowship in Architecture, and was in residence at the American Academy in Rome from 1954 to 1956. Kahn was a member of the jury that awarded the prize. Venturi refers to his time in Rome as a

visit to "architectural heaven."[16] His years in Italy influenced his architecture profoundly, and a number of buildings he saw there would have a direct bearing on the design of his mother's house. Venturi was interested in Borromini and in baroque and mannerist architecture. Especially important were Michelangelo's Porta Pia in Rome [fig.3] and the nymphaeum by Alessandro Vittoria in the rear garden of Palladio's Villa Barbaro at Maser [fig.4], both of the sixteenth century.[17] Venturi also discovered a modern-day Rome that few had bothered to look at. His formal as well as symbolic references for the house from twentieth-century Rome included the split pediment composition of Luigi Moretti's apartment building, Casa Girasole, on Via Parioli [fig.5] and the scenographic buildings of the elderly, then out-of-fashion architect Armando Brasini [fig.6].[18]

While in Rome, Venturi read for the first time Vincent Scully's *The Shingle Style and The Stick Style.*[19] One can only imagine his delight in comparing the architectural lessons of Rome to the numerous examples of the complex American shingle style [fig.7]. Scully's book provided another inspiration for the house: the great and near-to-the-ground pediment of McKim, Mead and White's Low House at Bristol, Rhode Island, of 1887 [fig.8]. Years later, Venturi's mother's house, along with the Willets House of 1911 by Frank Lloyd Wright, would be the only post-shingle style, twentieth-century buildings to be illustrated in Scully's revised edition of the book.

On his return from Rome in 1956, Robert worked in Louis Kahn's office for a brief nine-month period. He also accepted a position at the University of Pennsylvania as Kahn's teaching assistant. In Kahn's office he primarily worked on a conceptual megastructure project for Philadelphia. Venturi writes about Kahn that he was a "profound teacher of mine,

5

and ultimately, in some ways, as all teachers become, a student of mine."[20] In 1958, Venturi worked in association with Cope and Lippincott, and in 1960 he entered private practice with William Short as Venturi and Short.

In 1959 Robert, Sr., died at the age of seventy-eight. Vanna Venturi had moved from their house in suburban Rosemont to a series of apartments, but she decided to move to a small house, and purchased a flat, oddly shaped, three-quarter-acre lot on 8330 Millman Street in Philadelphia's suburban Chestnut Hill section. Coincidentally, it was across the street from Louis Kahn's recently constructed Esherick House [fig.9]. Venturi was thirty-four years old, and until then his designs had been primarily theoretical. Soon they would become concrete.

Like many parental commissions, Venturi's mother's house was designed to help the architect with his career; it was an opportunity to construct a building instead of writing and teaching about

6

them. Venturi was not to be a paper architect, and his first commission was not for a typical client. His mother trusted him to design without deadline, dialogue, or a detailed list of requirements. There was a plainness to the site and the program. This was to be no "dream house" in the grandiose sense. Vanna presented only a few guidelines: there was no need for a garage because she did not drive, her budget was modest, and she did not want the house to be pretentious.

Venturi began an odyssey that followed his interests. This house was to be his first building, and like many young architects, he was driven to test his ideas through construction. His college friend, the noted Shakespearean and Jacobean scholar Phillip Finkelpearl, recalls that "Bob was a lonely bachelor during those days. While living with his mother, he seemed to work every evening on the house as an almost desperate act to protect his own identity and express his architectural ideas." The next five years would

7, 8

prove to be one of the most fertile periods of his life. He was writing one of the most influential books on architecture, designing his first house, and dating the woman who would become his collaborator and wife.

While Venturi was formulating and teaching what was then the only course in America on architectural theory (and which became the foundation for his book *Complexity and Contradiction in Architecture*) at the University of Pennsylvania, he formed a friendship and academic collaboration with a young, British-trained professor from South Africa, Denise Scott Brown. "We were drawn together by being different from the rest of the faculty; we were bonded by being outsiders and not in the mainstream," recalls Venturi. She would visit his office at night and give advice on his designs; he would go to her design studio at Penn and critique her students. Scott Brown explains that his focus and shy, quiet manner were the subject of a five-year running joke among the students. "What does Venturi do all the time?" "He designs his mother's house." Denise Scott Brown and Venturi wrote:

The little house for a close friend or a relative is usually a first opportunity to test theories and expand them. If [the architect's] practice is slack, this at least allows him to put his heart and soul and a full work week into developing this one small idea, which is always a deepening experience. The years spent refining can be in the nature of a personal odyssey for the architect. It is an opportunity literally to seclude himself in order to focus his thinking.[21]

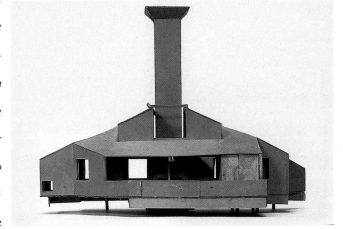

The drawings collected here represent the gestation of a theory of architecture. The five-year struggle that they chronicle describes a process of research and clarification. Even for this complex design, the progression of drawings displays Venturi's ability to simplify by discarding unsuccessful concepts and to start in new directions—an especially difficult and timely task for the young architect who wants to do it all in his first building.

The house went through six basic schemes, and six models exist that clearly exhibit the form of the house and the layers of his ideas. They identify Venturi's constant editing, which led to the superior final design. At the opening of The Museum of Modern Art's exhibition of the house in 1988, the models were displayed in chronological and descending order of size. Paul Goldberger, cultural editor of the *New York Times,* remarked, "It's a good thing Bob had five years to work on the house."[22]

The designs of the first four years followed a long and steady course, but a seemingly radical shift occurred in the year of the final design. Venturi explains, "The house was too large and too expensive, and in layman's terms, to economize, the square plan of the house was cut in half to form a rectangle that would cost considerably less."

Was it really that simple? Actually, after a four-year search, in the final design, there is a return to ideas first explored in his early theoretical Beach House, designed for himself in 1959 [fig.10]. Vincent Scully explains, "The principle of condensation becomes an extremely complex and interesting one. With the chimney rising through the gable, the general parti derives from that of the Beach House."[23] Vanna's house, after many alternatives, redirects its course to the design of an earlier project now influenced by his evolving ideas concerning shelter and symbolism. Even Venturi sees that now:

The house started out more like Kahn. After all, I was young and he was influential. The design was my way of learning and it was a wonderful experience. But I wasn't satisfied with the house and it didn't turn out the way I wanted it to be. In a way, I was lucky that the budget made the house change and it got much better. My intuition told me what to draw and took control of my hand. It told me what to do and it came out very quickly in the end.[24]

Vanna's house was to be Venturi's first building, but the design took so long that another commission was constructed first, the North Penn Visiting Nurses' Association Headquarters [fig.11] in Ambler, Pennsylvania (completed in 1961). If the North Penn building distorted the pure order of the box of modern architecture on the *outside* [fig.12], then the mother's house distorted it on the *inside* [fig.13]. Both buildings shared common ideas and illustrated his controversial thinking. Complex entries with symbolic, nonstructural, arched openings that organized the whole [fig.14], applied ornament, frames around windows [fig.15],[25] and conventional and big-scale elements expressed a new and complex architecture. Critics were dumfounded. "Where does this architecture go from here?" wrote the editors of *Architectural Forum* about the Nurses' Headquarters in the first magazine publication of a Venturi building.[26] Vanna's house held the answer.

The design was finally set. The construction drawings began

around Christmas 1962 and were completed in May 1963. Three consultants assisted with the work on the house: George Patton, landscape architect; Vinokur-Pace, mechanical and electrical engineers; and Keast and Hood, structural engineers. Venturi has continued to work with these firms throughout his career. The drawings and thirty-nine pages of specifications were given to Edmund A. Moyer, Sr., a contractor, who had successfully built Venturi's first building. Venturi and Moyer negotiated a price of $44,379 for a house of approximately eighteen hundred square feet.

Construction started in August 1963 and proceeded smoothly over a period of eight months, under the supervision of Venturi and John Rauch, his new partner at the time. Typical of any residential project, there were additions, clarifications, and refinements given to the contractor during construction, including the controversial stair to nowhere [fig.16], which does not appear on the working drawing set.[27] Venturi was pleased with the work of

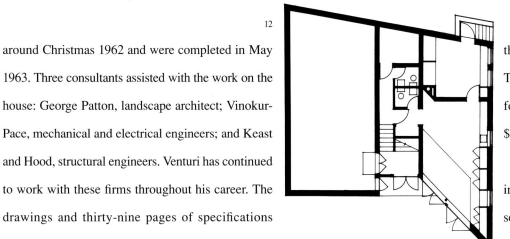

the contractor and they have remained friends. There were seventy-three items on the "punch list" for the contractor to remedy. The final cost was $54,430.16.

On April 1, 1964, Vanna and Robert moved into a house painted taupe grey, furnished with a selection of antiques and furniture from their previous homes. Venturi's almost "first" building was finally complete, except for one final stroke: in 1967, Robert painted the house pale green to make it "analogous" to its suburban location of trees and shrubs and because "there was a famous architect [Marcel Breuer] who said at the time, 'One thing I never do is use green on my houses because that's the color of nature and you never do that.' And I thought, good idea, and so I did it."[28]

Robert Venturi and Denise Scott Brown were married in 1967, and for a few months they lived upstairs in Vanna's house. Then they moved into an apartment building in Center City

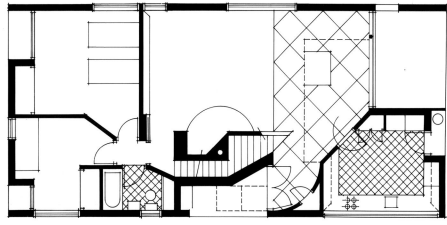

Philadelphia designed by I. M. Pei. Together they changed the course of modern architecture.[29] They also had a son named James.

Vanna Venturi was very happy in the house that her son designed and lived a secluded life there until 1973. Venturi recalls, "My mother loved the house. At first she thought the marble floor in the dining room was pretentious, but she was proud of it. She was a widow living alone, and she enjoyed showing the house to a lot of handsome young architects; she would sit them down at the dining room table and talk about Bernard Shaw—I assumed this was their price of admission."[30] Health problems later forced her into a nursing home, and she died in May 1975.

In 1973 Vanna's house was sold to Agatha and Thomas Hughes —she a distinguished potter and he the noted professor of the history of technology at the University of Pennsylvania. They have lovingly cared for the house and have lived there happily for the past nineteen years.

14

15

16

ILLUSTRATIONS

1. McKim, Mead and White, Pennsylvania Station, New York, New York, 1905–11, interior of central hall, by permission of the New York Historical Society

2. Vanbrugh and Hawksmoor, Blenheim Palace, Oxfordshire, England, 1705–24, front view, courtesy of Robert Venturi

3. Michelangelo, Porta Pia, Rome, Italy, circa 1562, courtesy of Robert Venturi

4. Alessandro Vittoria, nymphaeum, Villa Barbaro by Palladio, Maser, Italy, 1557–58, photo by Frederic Schwartz

5. Luigi Moretti, Casa Girasole, Rome, Italy, circa 1955, front view, photo by Cartoni, from Giuseppe Ungaretti, *50 Immagini di Architetture di Luigi Moretti*, de Luca Editore, Rome, 1968

6. Armando Brasini, Convento del Buno Pastore, near Rome, Italy, 1929–34, photo courtesy of Robert Venturi

7. Peabody and Stearns, "Kragsyde," Manchester-by-the-Sea, Massachusetts, circa 1882, from George William Sheldon, Artistic Country-Seats: *Villa and Cottage Architecture, with Instances of Country Clubhouses,* D. Appleton and Company, New York, 1889

8. McKim, Mead and White, Low House, Bristol, Rhode Island, 1887, photo by William F. Short, courtesy of Robert Venturi

9. Louis I. Kahn, Esherick House, Chestnut Hill, Philadelphia, Pennsylvania, 1959–61, rear elevation, photo by Ezra Stoller, by permission of ESTO

10. Robert Venturi, model, Beach House project, East Coast, America, 1959, rear elevation, photo courtesy of Venturi, Scott Brown and Associates

11. Venturi and Rauch, North Penn Visiting Nurses' Association Headquarters, Ambler, Pennsylvania, 1961, front view, photo by George Pohl, courtesy of Venturi, Scott Brown and Associates

12. Venturi and Rauch, North Penn Visiting Nurses' Association Headquarters, Ambler, Pennsylvania, 1961, ground floor plan, courtesy of Venturi, Scott Brown and Associates

13. Venturi and Rauch, Vanna Venturi House, Chestnut Hill, Philadelphia, Pennsylvania, 1964, ground floor plan, courtesy of Venturi, Scott Brown and Associates

14. Venturi and Rauch, North Penn Visiting Nurses' Association Headquarters, Ambler, Pennsylvania, 1961, entry, photo by George Pohl, courtesy of Venturi, Scott Brown and Associates

15. Venturi and Rauch, Vanna Venturi House, Chestnut Hill, Philadelphia, Pennsylvania, 1964, detail entry, photo by Rollin LaFrance, courtesy of Venturi, Scott Brown and Associates

16. Venturi and Rauch, Vanna Venturi House, Chestnut Hill, Philadelphia, Pennsylvania, 1964, stair, photo by Rollin LaFrance, courtesy of Venturi, Scott Brown and Associates

NOTES

1. Frank Lloyd Wright, "To the Young Man in Architecture," from "Two Lectures in Architecture, 1931," in *Frank Lloyd Wright: Writings and Buildings,* selected by Edgar Kaufman and Ben Reaburn (New York: Meridan Books, 1960).

2. Architecture is a collaborative act. The author recognizes the collective work and important contributions of Denise Scott Brown and the other members of the firm in the design process.

3. The best and first essay to include biographical information on the early years and career of Robert Venturi is Denise Scott Brown's "A Worm's Eye View of Recent Architectural History" in *Architectural Record* (February 1984): 69–81.

4. Robert Venturi, "Response at the Pritzker Prize Award Ceremony," at the Palacio de Iturbide, Mexico City, Mexico, May 16, 1991.

5. In 1975, while walking along the beach in Atlantic City, New Jersey, I met an old fisherman who asked me what I did. I said proudly, "I am studying to be an architect and working in Philadelphia for Venturi." He said, "Are you sure you don't sell fruit and vegetables?"

6. Robert Venturi, "Response at the Pritzker Prize Award Ceremony."

7. Robert Venturi, "Upbringing Among Quakers," in *Growing Up Italian* by Lida Brandi Cateura (New York: William Morrow and Company, 1987): 195–201. This is the best description of Venturi's family, early years, and Italian-American heritage.

8   Ibid., 197.

9   For his senior thesis, Venturi's designed a new building for the Théâtre Intime. His project was for a modern building in a traditional setting that would harmonize with its context. Looking back, Venturi says, he has been doing it ever since.

10 Robert Venturi, "Response at the Pritzker Prize Award Ceremony."

11 Robert Venturi, unpublished acceptance speech for the Madison Medal, Princeton University, February 16, 1985. For the best description of Venturi's education at Princeton, see also David Van Zanten, "The Princeton System and the Founding of the School of Architecture, 1915–20," *The Architecture of Robert Venturi* (Albuquerque, New Mexico: University of New Mexico Press, 1989): 34–44.

12 Robert Venturi, *Beaux-Arts Tradition in French Architecture* (Princeton, New Jersey: Princeton University Press, 1980): xiii.

13 George Howe is the designer of the PSFS Building, at the time the tallest and most important modern skyscraper in Philadelphia and a building that Venturi greatly admired.

14 Venturi's thesis for the master's degree was entitled "Context in Architectural Composition."

15 Robert Venturi, interview with the author, October 2, 1991.

16 Robert Venturi, "Response at the Pritzker Prize Award Ceremony."

17 Robert Venturi, "Diversity, Relevance and Representation in Historicism, or Plus ça Change . . . plus A Plea for Pattern all over Architecture, with a Postscript on My Mother's House," The Walter Gropius Lecture, Graduate School of Design, Harvard University, April 15, 1982, *Architectural Record* (June 1982): 114–119. (Venturi describes the role of classicism in the design of the house.)

18 Brasini's son credits Venturi as the first person to rediscover the important work of his father.

19 Vincent Scully, *The Shingle Style and The Stick Style* (New Haven, Connecticut: Yale University Press, 1955; revised edition, 1971).

20 Robert Venturi, "Response at the Pritzker Prize Award Ceremony."

21 Robert Venturi and Denise Scott Brown, "Some Houses of Ill-Repute." *Perspecta* 13/14 (Distributed by Wittenborn and Company, New York, 1969): 259.

22 An exhibition of the models of the house was held at The Museum of Modern Art, New York, New York in 1988. All six models of the house are in its permanent collection.

23 Vincent Scully, "Robert Venturi's Gentle Architecture," *The Architecture of Robert Venturi* (Albuquerque, New Mexico: University of New Mexico Press, 1989): 10.

24 Robert Venturi, interview with the author, October 2, 1991.

25 Venturi now tells a story of the then controversial frames around the windows at the North Penn Visiting Nurses' Headquarters. "A good friend of mine, who was an architect, came up to me one day and he put his arm around my shoulder and said, 'Bob, you know, I just want to give you some advice. You should never apply ornament in that way as borders around a window.' And I said, 'Okay, you're right.' Of course, inside, I was saying, 'Forget it, I'm right.' I mention that this architect now uses this device all over the place all the time."

26 "Pennsylvania Clinic," *Architectural Forum* (October 1963): 17.

27 Venturi acknowledges that the nowhere-stair was inspired specifically by a very small, almost non-stair that leads to the large tower of the Art and Architecture Library at the University of Pennsylvania by Frank Furness.

28 From undated lecture notes of Robert Venturi.

29 "Mr. Venturi and his wife and partner, Denise Scott Brown (co-author of much of his work since *Complexity and Contradiction in Architecture*), have together changed the way we see the world." Paul Goldberger, *New York Times*, August 14, 1991.

30 Michael Crosbie, "Venturi's House for his Mother Wins AIA 25-Year Award," *Architecture* (May 1989): 28; Robert Venturi, interview with the author, October 2, 1991.

ROBERT VENTURI

RESIDENCE IN CHESTNUT HILL

from *Complexity and Contradiction in Architecture*, 1966 [1]

This building recognizes complexities and contradictions: it is both complex and simple, open and closed, big and little; some of its elements are good on one level and bad on another—the order and the circumstantial elements of this house in particular. It achieves the difficult unity of a medium number of diverse parts rather than the easy unity of few or many motifs.

The inside spaces, as represented in plan and section, are complex and distorted in their shapes and interrelationships. They correspond to the complexities inherent in the domestic program as well as to some whimsies not inappropriate to an individual house. On the other hand, the outside form—as represented by the parapeted wall and the gable roof that enclose these complexities and distortions—is simple and consistent: it represents this house's public scale. The front, in its conventional combinations of door, windows, chimney, and gable, creates an almost symbolic image of a house.

The contradiction between inside and outside, however, is not total: inside, the plan as a whole reflects the symmetrical consistency of the outside; outside, the perforations in the elevations reflect the circumstantial distortions within. Concerning the inside, the plan is originally symmetrical with a central vertical core from which radiate two almost symmetrical diagonal walls that separate two end spaces in front from a major central space in back. This almost Palladian rigidity and symmetry is distorted, however, to accommodate the particular needs of the spaces: the kitchen on the right, for instance, varies from the bedroom on the left.

A more violent kind of accommodation occurs within the central core itself. Two vertical elements—the fireplace/chimney and the stair—compete, as it were, for central position. And each of these elements, one essentially solid, the other essentially void, compromises in its shape and position—that is, inflects—toward the other to make a unity of the duality of the central core they constitute. On one side the fireplace distorts in shape and moves over a little, as does its chimney; on the other side the stair suddenly constricts its width and distorts its path because of the chimney.

This core dominates as the center of the composition at this level; but at the level of its base, it is a residual element dominated itself by the spaces around it. On the living room side, its shape is rectangular and parallel to the important rectangular order of the important space there. Toward the front, it is shaped by a diagonal wall accommodating the also important and unique directional needs of the entrance space in its transition from big outer opening to inner entrance doors. The entrance space also competes for center position here. The stair, considered as an element alone in its awkward residual space, is bad; in relation to its position in a hierarchy of uses and spaces, however, it is a fragment appropriately accommodating a complex and contradictory whole, and as such it is good. From still another point of view, its shape is not awkward: at the bottom the stair is a place to sit, as well as to ascend, and to put objects later to be taken upstairs. And this stair, like those in shingle style houses, also wants to be bigger at its base to accommodate the bigger scale of the first floor. Similarly, the little "nowhere stair" from the second floor awkwardly accommodates its residual core space: on one level, it goes nowhere and is whimsical; at another level, it is like a ladder against a wall from which to wash the high window and paint the clerestory. The change in scale of the stair on this floor further contrasts with that change of scale in the other direction at the bottom.

The architectural complexities and distortions inside are reflected on the outside. The varying locations, sizes, and shapes of the windows and perforations on the outside walls, as well as the off-center location of the chimney, contradict the overall symmetry of the outside form: the windows are balanced on each side of the dominating entrance opening and chimney/clerestory element in the front, and the lunette window in the back, but they are asymmetrical. The protrusions above and beyond the rigid outside walls also reflect the complexity inside. The walls in front and back are parapeted to emphasize their role as screens behind which these inner intricacies can protrude. Indentations of the windows and porch on the sides, at all but one of the corners, increase the screenlike quality of the front and back walls in the same way as the parapets do at their tops.

When I called this house both open and closed as well as simple and complex, I was referring to these contradictory characteristics of the outside walls. First, their parapets along with the wall of the upper terrace in the back emphasize horizontal enclosure, yet permit an expression of openness behind them at the upper terrace and above them at the chimney/clerestory protrusion. Second, the consistent shape of the walls in plan emphasizes rigid enclosure, yet the big openings, often precariously close to the corners, contradict the expression of enclosure. This method of walls—layered for enclosure, yet punctured for openness—occurs vividly at the front center, where the outside wall is superimposed upon the two other walls housing the stair. Each of these three layers juxtaposes openings of differing size and position. Here is layered space rather than interpenetrated space.

The house is big as well as little, by which I mean that it is a little house with big scale. Inside the elements are big: the fireplace is "too big" and the mantel "too high" for the size of the room; doors are wide, the chair rail high. Another manifestation of big scale inside is a minimum of subdivisions of space; also for the sake of economy, the plan minimizes purely circulation space. Outside the manifestations of big scale are the main elements, which are big and few in number and central or symmetrical in position, as well as the simplicity and consistency of the form and silhouette of the whole, which I have already described. In back, the lunette window is big and dominating in its shape and position. In front, the entrance loggia is wide, high, and central. Its big scale is emphasized by its contrast with the other doors, smaller in size yet similar in shape; by its shallowness for its size, and by the expedient position of the inner entrance behind it. The applied wood molding over the door increases its scale, too. The dado increases the scale of the building all around because it is higher than you expect it to be. These moldings affect the scale in another way also: they make the stucco walls even more abstract, and the scale, usually implied by the nature of materials, more ambiguous or noncommittal.

The main reason for the large scale is to counterbalance the complexity. Complexity in combination with small scale in small buildings means busyness. Like the other organized complexities here, the big scale in the small building achieves tension rather than nervousness—a tension appropriate for this kind of architecture.

The setting of the house is a flat, open, interior site, enclosed at its boundaries by trees and fences. The house sits near the middle, like a pavilion, with no planting near it. The driveway axis, perpendicular to the middle of the house, is distorted in its position by the circumstantial location of a sewer main at the curb of the street.

The abstract composition of this building almost equally combines rectangular, diagonal, and curving elements. The rectangles relate to the dominant order of the spaces in plan and section. The diagonals relate to directional space at the entrance, to particular relationships of the directional and nondirectional spaces within the rigid enclosure on the first floor, and to the enclosing and water-shedding functions of the roof. The curves relate to the directional/spatial needs at the entry and outside stair, to spatial-expressive needs in section in the dining room ceiling, which is contradictory to the outside slope of the roof, and to the symbolism of the entrance and its big scale, which is produced by the molding on the front elevation. The exceptional point in the plan refers to the expedient column support, which contrasts with the otherwise wall-bearing structure of the whole. These complex combinations do not achieve the easy harmony of a few motifs based on exclusion—based, that is, on "less is more." Instead, they achieve the difficult unity of a medium number of diverse parts based on inclusion and on acknowledgment of the diversity of experience.

NOTE

[1] Robert Venturi, *Complexity and Contradiction in Architecture* (New York: The Museum of Modern Art Papers on Architecture, in association with the Graham Foundation for the Advanced Studies in the Fine Arts, Chicago, 1966), pp. 117–121, by permission of The Museum of Modern Art.

ROBERT VENTURI

MOTHER'S HOUSE 25 YEARS LATER

It is hard to remember, or at least sense, how things were twenty-five years ago. What seemed extraordinary then seems ordinary now—or vice versa. This kind of misreckoning occurs especially in matters of taste where we see yesterday in the context of today and through the eyes of today; within our current sensibility the remote past looks old and the recent past, old-fashioned. Have you ever noticed how outrageously short (or long) ladies' skirts look in old photographs and then wondered how you did not go around thinking at the time how strange skirts looked? And if you are too young to remember twenty-five years ago, understanding the recent past is particularly difficult, curiously more difficult than in the case of the distant past. This certainly applies to architecture where not only yesterday's extraordinary may have become today's ordinary, but yesterday's outrage today's cliche. I recall driving past Guild House recently with an acquaintance who expressed wonder at what all the fuss had been about—at how this building's explicitly ordinary vocabulary and its scale-augmenting central motif, now on almost every skyscraper designed in the last decade—had seemed outrageous when it was built.

Now that it is twenty-five years old, the architecture of my mother's house is accepted and its originality tends to be forgotten. This means it has been influential, though not always to good effect, of course. Many of its elements have become trademarks of so-called postmodernism.

You can see this house all over the world in different contexts and combinations, sometimes forty stories up capping high-rise buildings. And if the building now seems a little obvious and is condescended to, I remember how it was originally ignored or scorned; we tend now to forget how sure of themselves the modernists were in their almost religious fervor. (An exception to these kinds of reactions was Ellen Perry Berkeley's understanding critique, published in *Progressive Architecture* when the house was built.)

So the early bird went too far and hasn't gone far enough. But more important, I remember how hard this building was for me to arrive at. It hurts while you are going against the grain; four years of a lot of agony and very little ecstasy.

I originally described it as a small building with big scale. When I wrote about it in *Complexity and Contradiction* I stressed its mannerism—its complexities and contradictions. Now I refer as well to its symbolism. That I saw and explained the house differently then from now is not a bad thing; it means its architecture has dimensions and makes sense from several perspectives.

Some ordinary/extraordinary elements of the building are:

— The window as a hole in the wall. In modern architecture, the ideal was not a hole in the wall, which negated the integrity of the wall, but an interruption of wall, an absence of wall, which promoted flowing space and abrogated enclosed space. In late modern architecture, if a window *was* actually a hole in the wall, it was camouflaged by spandrels above and below or by wide piers at the sides; in the late work of Louis Kahn, there were open holes in the wall but never conventional windows.

— The window as symbol. The vertical and horizontal muntins of most windows in the house produced panes that reminded you of traditional or conventional windows. This was particularly outrageous in the 1960s, and it took a lot of doing to insert the horizontal muntin in the aluminum frame sliding doors to make them look like windows. This squarish window with four panes is everywhere now; it is an important theme in the work of Aldo Rossi. But it is hard to conceive how outrageous its use as a symbol seemed at first to most architects and critics.

— The pediment. Like the window, this was unusual then and is typical now. A sloped roof was okay in those days as long as it was a shed roof. But the main facade where two slopes met to form a pediment contravened a taboo. The pediment was again both too familiar and too old-fashioned, too rare and too outrageous. And because pediments are quintessentially classical, it raised a symbolic issue too.

— Yet this pediment, being on the long facade, is also anticlassical. This is one place where this house is mannerist. The pediment used in this fashion becomes a sign, a kind of representation of a classical composition.

— Dados. Decorative moldings were out in the 1960s. In my mother's house the dado molding on the facade further promoted classical references and, because it was placed unusually high, it created a generous scale for a small building. The chair-rail molding inside (also unusually high) was never used then either.

— Scale. This quality of little building and big scale was further enhanced by the superimposition of the big entrance opening over the normal-sized door beyond.

— Arches that are symbolic and not structural. Arches in modern architecture could only be manifestations of structural vaults behind. In this house there is an arched lunette window in the back and a curved molding over the entrance opening in the front. The lunette is a device often used in neoclassical architecture to enhance the scale of a two-story

house by making it look one story high, and the arch molding at the front symbolizes entrance. Again, the classical symbolism was taboo: arches as structural expression, yes; arches as symbolic meaning, no.

— Distorted symmetry. Some symmetry had returned to functionalist modernism by the early 1960s in the work of Mies van der Rohe and Louis Kahn, but distorting the symmetry was out. You couldn't have it both ways: if an order was right it should not have to be compromised. Aalto's work was the exception in the 1960s.

— Redundancy. The arch molding in front was overlaid on a flush concrete beam to contrast with this element's literal structural quality. Besides being a stuck-on decorative pastiche, the molding was outrageous for its expressive redundancy. In those days, structural efficiency and expressive minimalism, yes; ambiguous meaning and complexity of expression, no. But I loved the Porta Pia.

— Enclosure. Although the early International Style had acknowledged enclosed interior space with windows or holes puncturing exterior walls as in Mies van der Rohe's Afrikaner Strasse housing or even Le Corbusier's Villa Savoye, other directions had prevailed by the late-modern 1960s, following, for example, Mies's directed and flowing space of the Barcelona Pavilion or Corb's vast lobbies made up of walls and absences of walls. Enclosure was out, corners were taboo. My mother's house returned to enclosed interior space with windows.

— Shelter. The house is a shelter as well as an enclosure. The flat roofs of modern architecture, and particularly of the parapeted Villa Savoye, kept the rain out but didn't suggest shelter. In my mother's house, the pedimented roof symbolized shelter as well as classicism.

— Color. I made the house green in 1967. Although trim could be colored in those days, surface material had to be natural to express the nature of the material and structure. Green was out.

— Furniture. I designed the house so my mother's old furniture (c. 1925, plus some antiques) would look good in it. In those days interiors were expected to be purely modern. Although you could scatter some very old antiques about (and the Italians were masters at this), eclecticism was essentially out.

— Sign and symbol. Orthodox modern architects, without admitting it, employed symbolism; they denounced historical symbolism but promoted the "progressive" symbols of industry. Their adaptation of industrial elements, frequently without regard for context, was mainly in the details; the buildings, as wholes, didn't look like factories. In contrast, my mother's house, while it employed certain historical/classical details, stressed the symbolic significance of the building as a whole. In its sheltering manner, with its gable roof, central door, ordinary windows and

chimney, it looked like an elemental house, like a child's drawing of a house. It was also a sign, because the gable was on the long facade and because the parapet caused the facade to seem detached from the house. This made the representational quality of the house more explicit.

— Originality. In those days a house had to be original to be good. This house was original, but not in the modern sense of expressing the new.

— Ideology. The house did not promote ideology. My architectural approach was not pure. The house is both not modern and modern: although it has corners, it also doesn't have corners; it has a steel frame strip window and there is an absence of wall, not a hole in the wall, between the dining area and the porch. Its inconsistency makes it hard to categorize. It is not postmodern. The inside *feels* Corbusian; the steel column and what it supports seem like an International Style reference.

— Classical and elemental qualities. To me, the most unusual characteristics of this building now are its classicism and its elemental quality. It is classical in that it is explicitly symmetrical in its plan and major elevations. The symmetry builds up toward the center through a hierarchical arrangement of elements and an increase of scale. The symmetry is not incidental as in, for instance, some of Mies van der Rohe's buildings, which are made up of repetitive modular elements. Of course the classicism is mannerist because of the inconsistency of its symmetry. (Our next building, Guild House, created an hierarchical center and a contrast of scales on the front elevation, using connected balconies capped by a lunette window—a compositional device now characteristic of many postmodern high-rise buildings.) The same house is also elemental in that it can be read as an archetype—the child's image of house.

It took several years of struggle to evolve this house, as is demonstrated here in Frederic Schwartz's book, and the struggle involved discarding a series of good ideas, or having to postpone employing them for future work, which is always difficult for a young architect. Its final design returned to a degree ironically close to my earlier Beach House design in its form if not its symbolic or referential content; that is, the Beach House was maybe the first shingle style revival building, the latter, the first so-called postmodern building. But I have lived off this building, which took so long to be born, ever since, and so have others, I think, consciously or unconsciously.

Thomas and Agatha Hughes have been the possessors of the house since 1973, and I want to thank them for their care and understanding in living in their house and maintaining it.

Philadelphia, 1991

VINCENT SCULLY

EVERYBODY NEEDS EVERYTHING

First Russian student, on the Vanna Venturi house: "Who needs it?"

Second student: "Everybody needs everything."

Leningrad, 1965

Robert Venturi's little house for Vanna Venturi, designed 1959–63 and built in 1963–64, has turned out to be the biggest small building of the second half of the twentieth century. It has been big in its effects, in its initiation not only of the vernacular and classical revivals of the past thirty years, but also of the abstractly theoretical architecture of the same period. It is also big in itself, in the archetypal order of its form. Its facade is a diagram of that order. And even if only its facade were known, or if in fact there were no building behind it, that diagram would still have a telling effect because it is a perfect drawing, weightless as pure line and transcending material, of Neoplatonic order imposed upon or growing out of human life: hence the asymmetrical windows of various sizes, but all functions of the square, which slide across it. These do not destroy but underscore and enliven the essential and purely geometric shapes of the facade: the triangle, the circle, and the square, here in fact a near-square, all drawn taut as wire. They are indeed handled as line drawing on paper. Who would guess that the wall they shape is in fact built of plastered cinder block? It is carefully made to look like a cutout cardboard model of a curious color, associated with no material. All the modernist cant, rooted in nineteenth-century materialism, about the "expression of materials," is not simply honored in the breach, which was often the modernist way, but overtly cast aside, much as Le Corbusier had done in the early 1920s.

The entrance facade of Le Corbusier's Stein Villa at Garches [fig.1], for example, is treated as pure screen, linear and weightless but perforated at its upper level to reveal the shapes of a bathroom swelling outrageously behind it. Like Le Corbusier, Venturi is stretching the European aesthetic of the Ideal to its uttermost limits, or reducing it to its essentials, which reside in the line drawing of perfect geometric shapes. Venturi's facade is not transparent like Le Corbusier's, but

1

it goes further than his in focusing upon the most pervasive and essential Neoplatonic image of all, which is that of the human figure placed in the center of the circle and the square. It is the Vitruvian vision [fig.2], drawn hundreds of times throughout the Middle Ages and the Renaissance and no less essential to the development of Gothic architecture than it was to that of the Renaissance. Venturi taps directly into that Ideal power, and in a rather baroque or perhaps a modern way he makes it more dynamic. The central opening looks square but is in fact rectangular. It is a pure void, emerging directly from the ground upon whose plane the human figure rests while the circle bursts apart around it, seeming to explode outward from the human being in the center and, by extension, arcing down into the earth as well. The image becomes even more embracing; the figure at its center more powerful.

And here Venturi works his great switch. All previous embodiments of human centrality in this diagram had been of the heroic male figure, an athletic, aggressive being who fits into but basically dominates the essential shapes of the world. But here it is Vanna Venturi, seated in her kitchen chair with a pot of geraniums beside her. She is tiny, but the space detonates around her. Directly above her head

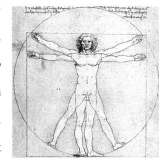
2

the gable splits to release her energy beyond the circle and the square to the empyrean. Here the rich balance of opposites, or complementaries, which was to shape all of Venturi's later work, achieved its first and still its most compelling image. Contrasted with the traditional male figure, Vanna Venturi is at once anti-heroic and feminist in meaning. She is stronger than he; at rest, she breaks the mold. It was this combination of subversive attitudes that caused so many architects of the 1960s to hate Robert Venturi so earnestly. He was striking at their heroic image of themselves as godlike creators, an idea fundamentally ridiculous in itself and dangerous to architecture but one which was deeply rooted in romanticism and which late modernism had done everything to encourage. The fact that Vanna Venturi was Robert Venturi's mother fueled the fires. Everybody knew all about mothers in 1960. It was risky for a male to admit that he had ever had one. The truth is that the macho pretensions of architects have always rested upon rather shaky foundations in the modern period. Such could easily be read in the early sixties in their destructive urbanism and brutalist constructions alike [fig.3]. Modernism had trapped them in an unreal and untenable mythology from which they needed release very badly. Venturi went to the heart of the matter with his gentle feminist image, a harbinger of healthier things to come.

3

Behind Vanna Venturi the void of the square opens to a further subversion of the ideal order of the facade, much as Le Corbusier had done in his bathroom at the Stein Villa. So Venturi shows us an interior as if in tumult behind the frontal plane, with a false stair rising to infinity above the second floor, like the ladder of Jacob's dream mounting to heaven. Below that apparition the entrance void opens to the right to show us the hidden front door, beyond which the interior spaces are all easily and asymmetrically adjusted to each other. How easy indeed it all seems: the curved wall on entry, the chair rail leading us along, the coved ceiling over the dining table recalling the exterior circle, the fireplace pushed over by the staircase and inflected back toward the main space, the stair itself contracted and expanded, making the most of its opportunities for drama, the bedroom "under the eaves," the boy's room (again driving the critics crazy), the stair to heaven, finally the little parapeted balcony at the rear, where everything is the reverse of the front. A wide flat arch stretches across and contains the volume of the house in contrast to the detached split gable of the other side. Here we are even allowed to see that the building embraces three dimensions. There is a moderately scaled chimney in the middle; it had been made to look like a flat plane, simply part of the facade, on the entrance side. Still, the walls remain thin; the little porch by the dining room denies the house a closed corner at that point, and that International Style reference is enhanced by the pipe railing of the basement stair.

Surely there was never a building so in love with the complexities and contradictions of architecture and with its own immediate architectural past, with modernism. As Philip Johnson's Glass House [fig.4] was in one distinct way the ultimate modern building—reduced, that is, to a frame for the individual in nature—so Venturi's was the other distinctly modern statement, one totally affected by the complexity of the modern condition and the availability of historical data and therefore wanting to try everything with which the contemporary human brain is stored. That complexity is what makes the genesis of its design so interesting, more interesting at the moment than its effects, which are, as noted above, well known.

The ancestry of the Vanna

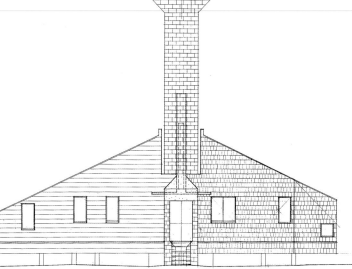

Venturi House once seemed clear enough. First came Venturi's great project for a Beach House. of 1959 [fig.5] with its vast, shingled, frontal gable derived from that of McKim, Mead and White's Low House of 1887 [fig.6], and its outrageous chimney, adapted from those of Sir Edwin Lutyens at Middlefield of 1908 [fig.7], and with more than a touch of the Villa Savoye of 1929–31 [fig.8] in its thin skin, horizontal voids, and pilotis. From the Beach House it seemed a direct step to the frontal gable of the Vanna Venturi House, with its echoes of Frank Lloyd Wright's own house of 1889 [fig.9], even in the Neo-Vitruvian half circle pasted on the facade. Moreover, Robert Stern had published a few early studies of the Vanna Venturi design in his unique *Perspecta 9/10* of 1965 (pp.38–39) and, while these differed in plan from the final version, exhibiting as they did squarish, separate rooms of a kind Venturi has always acknowledged as Louis I. Kahn's, they were otherwise of a type stressing the relationship to the Beach House, to

6

7

8

9

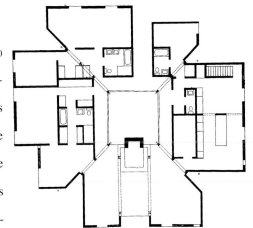

its chimney and gable. So both of Venturi's important early designs seemed to be direct spin-offs from the climactic years of the Shingle Style of the 1880s, with only moderate indications of influence from the work of Kahn, in whose office Venturi was employed for nine highly fraught months, beginning in September 1956. Perhaps there was also some reflection of the plan of Kahn's Goldenberg House project of 1959 [fig.10] in the Beach House and some sanction for its monumental shingled gable in Kahn's powerful pyramidal roofs at Trenton of 1955. But the Vanna Venturi House itself seemed wholly foreign to Kahn's work, and its gable, traditionally expressive of "house," indeed stands in firm contrast to the abstract, flat-roofed boxes of Kahn's Esherick House, of 1959-61 [fig.11], just up the road. But now that Venturi has released the relevant drawings for publication—a long series beginning, it would seem, in 1959—it becomes apparent that the design for the Vanna Venturi House did not at all begin as a simple progression from the Beach House project. It is obvious, on the con-

trary, that Venturi started with some elements that were his own and some that were Kahn's and wrestled with that mixture through years of drawings. These leave a record of the struggle of antagonists loving and fearing each other, coming out only toward the last with something that was almost wholly new, and Venturi's own, with accreted experiences purged away or fused into his own being. In the process, curiously, Venturi seems to have passed through stations on the road through Kahn's work, and his own, where many less driven individuals were to come to rest—Giurgola, Botta, and many others as well. Beyond that, the sequence of drawings recalls Wright's relationship to Sullivan from 1887 to 1893, deeply emotional on both sides, ending in the rejection of the younger man by the older, in which the forms original to the apprentice and to the master are not always easy to define.

The sequence begins with a group of drawings from Venturi's archives which illustrate a masonry project of concrete block and heavy concrete lintels. On the ground floor, one

12

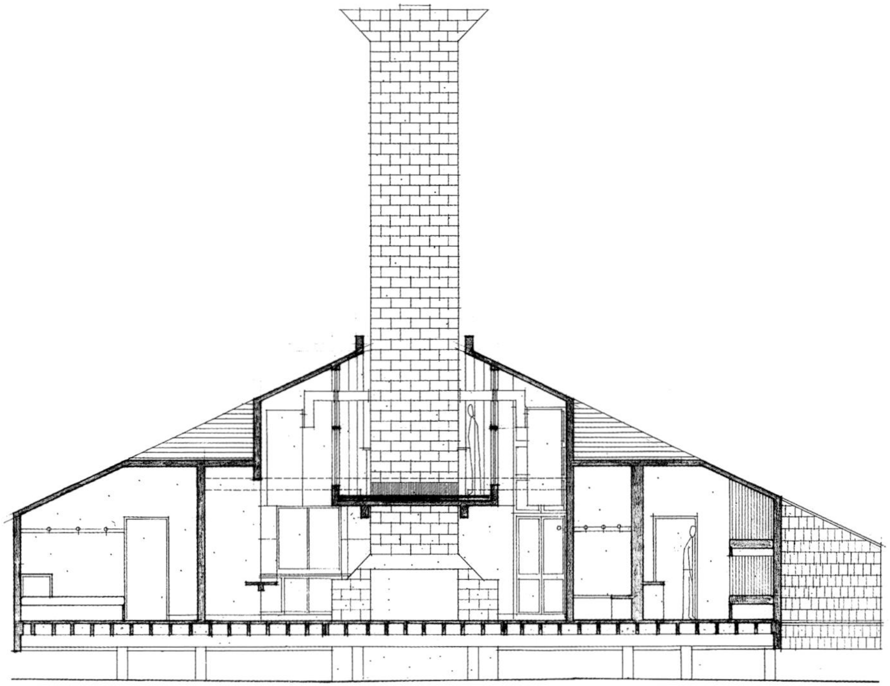

thinks as much of the late Le Corbusier as of Kahn, but up above the design bursts into a welter of roof shapes expressive of elaborate schemes for encapsulating discrete interior spaces and lighting them from above. They seem typical of Kahn at his most obsessed. Yet when we look at the date we must pause because the urge to light spaces from above, indeed to design in section, comes to Kahn only later and is most beautifully developed in his later museums. Venturi himself believes that the sectional preoccupation and the overhead lighting are his own and derive from his personal experience of the oculi and thermal windows of Rome. Above everything else in this first project, Venturi's own obsessive chimney looms. It is clearly the architect's central love at the moment, his image of his own individuality—which he seems determined at this point to make more macho than that of his colleagues. (One can hardly help but

13

recall Melville's story *I and My Chimney*, about a man who defends the central chimney mass of his colonial house from his wife and daughters, who are convinced it is structurally faulty, as well as terribly in the way, and want to tear it down.) Hence the chimney is the single feature of this design that is shared with the Beach House project [fig.12]. The section (Scheme I/**6**, p.66) shows high, coved spaces, light monitors, and skyscraper flues. Even what we have come to think of as Kahn's "ruins wrapped around buildings," which first appear in his work in the first design for the U.S. Consulate in Luanda, Angola, of 1959–62, are there in the section to set up a deep spatial layering for the main facades [fig.13]. But again there is a critical question of date here. Kahn's ruins don't stand free of his enclosing walls until his project for the Salk Community Center of 1961–62 [fig.14]; Venturi's drawings of this first

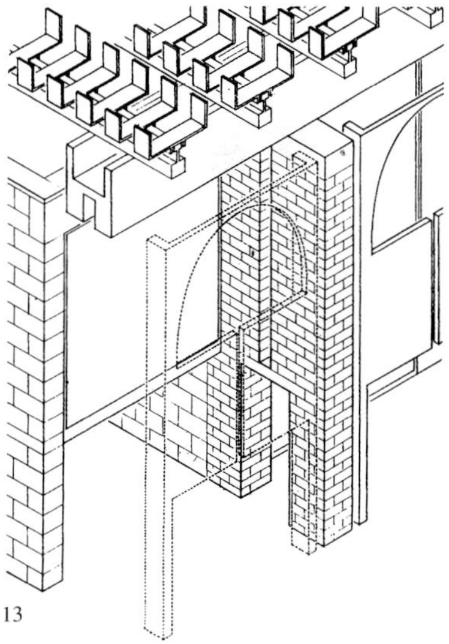

Vanna Venturi project are earlier than that, so that Venturi's layering would seem to be entirely his own, not derivative from Kahn's. It clearly pre-dates Kahn's in any event. Venturi himself traces it back to his earliest projects and ascribes it, again, to Rome, specifically to Brasini's Forestry Building at the E.U.R. of 1942, now demolished [fig.15]. Moreover, Stern's *Perspecta 9/10* (pp. 50–51) also published a project for a "House at Chestnut Hill" (known also as the Pearson House) by Venturi, dated 1957 [fig.16, 17], where the layering of ruins far out in space was already conspicuously present. Its plan, though strung out, also resembles that of some of the early plans of the Vanna Venturi project published by Stern, but what is apparently the first plan for that project, never before published, now comes as something of a shocker. It is pure Kahn, and the Kahn of the Fleischer project of 1959 [fig.18], not of the much less characteristic Goldenberg House, which Venturi himself, however, specifically identifies as Kahn's as well. Curiously, Venturi vividly remembers the Goldenberg plan but

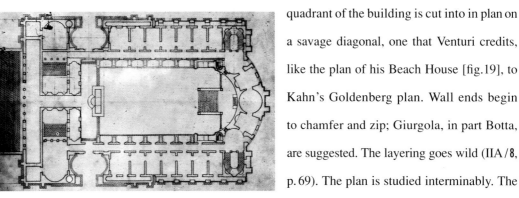

not the Fleischer one. But the Vanna Venturi plan, like the Fleischer, is rigidly cubical, stiff, and basically symmetrical; each space is a discrete structure, while out beyond the main facade the ruins rather dementedly stand. Then it is shown on the site. slightly canted off the major axes of road and lot, thus arbitrarily avoiding its natural placement as all the other early site plans were also to do.

Side elevations follow and begin to be reworked on their own. A slanted roof slips in and all the forms begin to simplify somewhat below it. The layered walls disappear. The section is stronger and clearer; the chimney still rides high, but then the whole mass is cut into again, cut down, lowered, and made more modest. But now something new intrudes. One quadrant of the building is cut into in plan on a savage diagonal, one that Venturi credits, like the plan of his Beach House [fig.19], to Kahn's Goldenberg plan. Wall ends begin to chamfer and zip; Giurgola, in part Botta, are suggested. The layering goes wild (IIA/**8**, p. 69). The plan is studied interminably. The

16

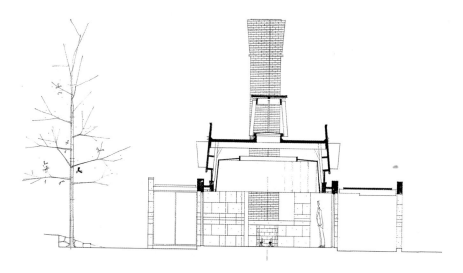

17

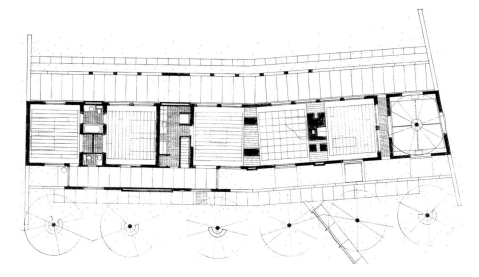

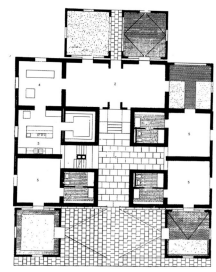

18

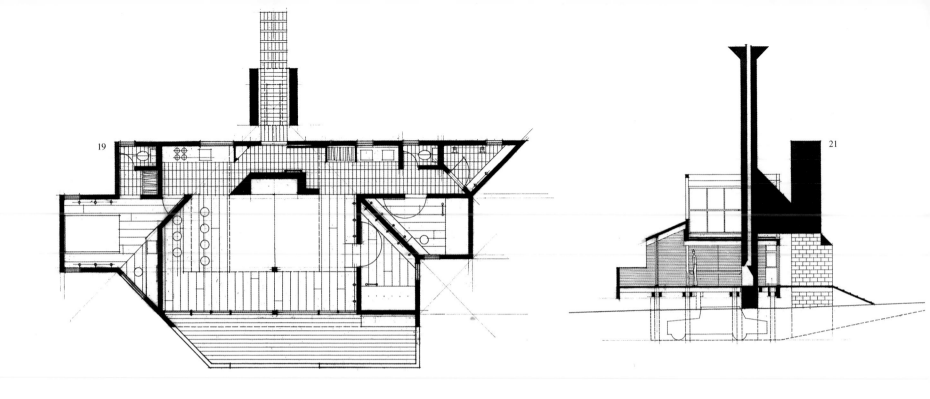

19

21

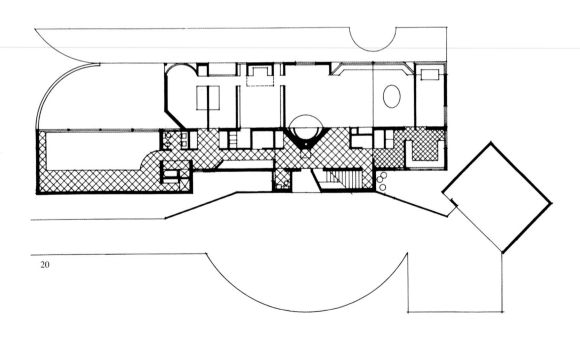

20

48.

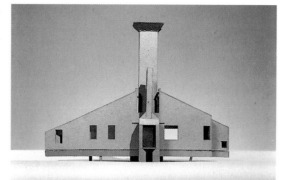

22

fireplaces become ever more complex monuments in the center: they are grottoes, caverns, towers. The structure is always of block masonry, solid, structurally demanding, shaping very separate spaces that are essentially dominated by it. The screening walls reappear and various complicated monitors proliferate above. The block pattern of the masonry walls remains of major concern, as do the medieval flues (IIC/**29**, p. 92) and the canted placement on the lot (IIC/**22**, p. 85). The thing continues to rotate on the lot (IIIA/**31**, p. 98). It begins to want to sprout an enclosed court; this was to remain a preoccupation almost to the last. It also appeared in Venturi's eloquent scheme for the Millard Meiss House of 1962 [fig.20], which was produced when the sequence of design here had just been completed, and which suggests the earlier Kahn-like plans and especially those of the project of 1957 published by Stern.

      The study plans for the Vanna Venturi House are endless.

Slowly they begin to compact, to simplify, and to become less symmetrical; the zips and zaps tend to turn into projected planes of wall. Then the Beach House chimney [fig.21, 22] reappears in its original form (IIIB/**44**, p.115), bursting up the center much as its precursors had done. The flues are room size. Soon, however, the chimney thins out and leaps much higher, as if in the paroxysm of approaching death, and for the first time (at least in this numbered sequence, where some drawings may well have ended up out of strictly chronological order in Venturi's archives), a half-round window appears, enormous in scale. This, of course, had been a central feature of Wright's house, and of numerous gables by Jefferson before him. Palladio had used it on the entrance facades of several villas [fig.23], where its derivation was from the high windows of Roman baths. Kahn probably got it directly from Hadrian's Villa or from one of the other Roman ruins so essential

23

to his later work, to which he was led in 1950–51 by the great classicist of the American Academy in Rome, the late Frank E. Brown. The round arch in strikingly Roman guise was indeed the major space maker and room shaper of Kahn's Fleischer project [fig.24], arching up in four planes to model a separate canopied volume over each room. By 1960 it had also played a decisive part in Venturi's design for Guild House [fig.25] as well. And the facade of that building clearly owed a direct debt to Kahn's Luanda project [fig.26] and to the project for the Salk Community Center [fig.27], in which the outer layer of "ruin" is at once integrated with the building and expressed as a freestanding plane, pierced by a half-round opening. Yet that thermal window was Venturi's, too, part of his own direct legacy from Rome.

It would seem that the arched windows attracted Venturi as the natural opposite of the chimney—spatial rather than sculptural, sheltering rather than aggressive. Otherwise, for a while the designs are all Low House (IIIA / 33–36, pp.100–103; IIIB / 40–42, pp.111–113) but the gables remain masonry block. The chimney continues to jump up and down but begins to become rather ghostly in effect, drawn in thin outline as if about to disappear. It is obviously beginning to lose its symbolic hold on Venturi, perhaps without his own full awareness of the change, because all of a sudden, though still elaborate, the fireplaces are no longer in the center; they are pushed toward one side and the plan is enormously simplified. Clearly the idea of a second floor has begun to come into play (IVB / 57, p.134). Hence the monitor structure for the first floor rooms can no longer be maintained, and the thrust of the chimney must concomitantly dwindle.

Venturi fiddles with these new ideas. In section, the design begins for the first time to resemble the final project a little (IVB / 66, p.143). The fireplace is leaning. The round arch is lifting as a big window (IVB / 65, p.142); it is killing off the chimney at last. A containing void, now rather simply conceived, is winning out over thrusting mass and monumental structure—which is still, however, of masonry blocks. But there a shift now occurs (IVB / 62, p.139). The lintels are bigger; there is less insistence on the block, at least in some drawings. A stair is seen in profile through a window, and a chopped-off three quarters of a circle, like some used by Venturi later, is experimented with (IVB / 63, p.140).

25

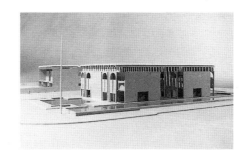

26   27

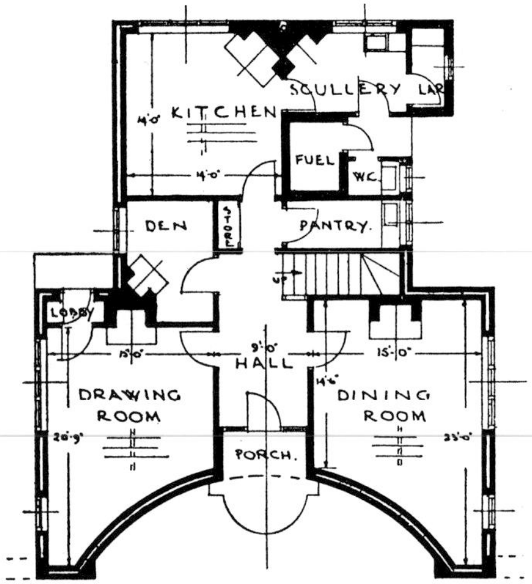

The block is still there, but the volume is stretching, so that the lintels seem to be stretching too, as if beginning to feel the lateral spatial pressure to which the lintel as finally built on the facade so tautly responds. The windows, as well, are close to the final examples; they are turning square and getting cross-mullioned. It is all thinning out, becoming much less structurally obsessive. When will he get rid of the blocks, we ask.

The plan itself is rushing rapidly toward the final version (V/68, p.148). The Lutyens-like void before the entrance door appears, along with Lutyens's typical curved walls avoiding edges within [fig.28]. One room is tiled; there is an upstairs eyrie with bath (IVB/66, p.143), all much more modest than the earlier upstairs bedrooms. Clearly, budgetary limitations, the young architect's best friends, are beginning to play a part. They, or his own classical sense of decorum, which he was to develop so effectively later, are helping Venturi enormously here. Grandiose ideas and ancient obsessions are fading. We are getting down to the wire. "Do this plan all over," says one drawing (V/69, p.149). The sections (V/74, p.154; V/75, p.155) are close to final realiza-

tion. There is a true spatial economy and unity that the early versions lacked. There is no duplication; everything acts with maximum valence, rising now not to the aggressive sculptural mass of a chimney but to the arched window of the upper room. Then the rear elevation (V/72, p.152) is fixed; the essentials are almost there; they only need to be proportioned. But there is still the block, and the whole thing continues to roll drunkenly on the site. This version is studied further in plan and elevation.

Finally, a decisive shift in emphasis occurs: from now on, no masonry block is drawn. It is still there as structure, apparently, but is now stuccoed over, and the elevations are studied as line and volume. The drawings are now uniformly gentle; the time for aggressive assertion seems past. The solids are indicated only minimally, as if simply to define spaces, but the symbolic clarity of their shapes is stronger than ever, as is their archetypal geometry. It is as if Venturi had worked his way through all the inessential *sturm und drang* of late modernism to come out at last into a reasonable, peaceful pool of space and symbol, spiritually simple, certain, and strong, needing to pump no iron.

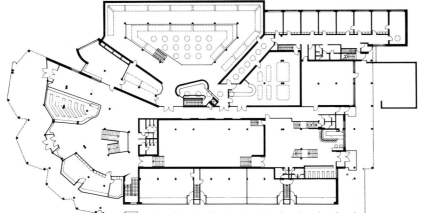

29

With the section drawing (VI/**78**, p.161) we are fundamentally there. The design is almost fixed; most of all, perhaps, the house has now come to rest on the lot, facing the entrance drive—though oh-so-correctly kept off the central axis—and lining up with the orthogonals of the ground shape. The plan is almost ready, too; the major spaces are in place, but their peculiarly genial flow from one to the other has not yet been worked out (VI/**79**, p.162). So Venturi tries loosening up the kitchen (VI/**80**, p.163), and then moves on in that rhythm to unite the whole thing; working with circles to resonate off the entrance arc, the stair coming alive, the two bedrooms adjusting to the circulation and each other (VI/**82**, p.165). It is all turning into his own kind of planning, flexible and resourceful, imprisoned in no geometric scheme. It now seems to owe nothing essential to Kahn, though surely something to Aalto [fig.29] and Lutyens [fig.30] and to the young Le Corbusier [fig.31] as well, and it was

30

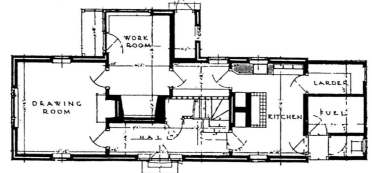

to take on a special kind of casual force in Venturi's later work.

The final scheme is solidly dimensioned at last (VI/**81**, p.164), but Venturi jumps to modify the living room wall. The upstairs room takes on its definitive shape (VI/**89**, p.172) and establishes its relationship to the ghost stair and to the window-of-appearances behind the facade. Sections and elevations, mainly pure line, now try to work out the final relationships between the chimney and the roof. Then it is done, and we get all the neatly dimensioned drawings. How moving it is to witness the dénouement of the process, to this point highly personal, when the architect sits down to make it all materially real and, most of all, to communicate it clearly to the builder. Even the thin structure of the fence shaping the courtyard on the side is drawn, but will never be constructed. The facade is studied in three drawings (VI/**91**, p.174; VI/**93**, p.176; VI/**94**, p.177) that were rather naughtily sold, with others, to the Deutsches Architekturmuseum in Frankfurt.

The first has a rectangular central opening, pronouncedly horizontal with a column stuck in it. The other two both study the application of an arched strip to the facade over the opening and seem to eliminate the column. The arch springs from what appears to be pilasters framing the opening, which is itself now approaching a square shape. No drawing which has yet surfaced quite prepares us for the finished entrance facade, where the fragment of the circle—the descendant of Vitruvius and Palladio and forebear of a thousand similar appliqués—leaps free of the near-square below it to suggest the whole Neoplatonic circle wheeling

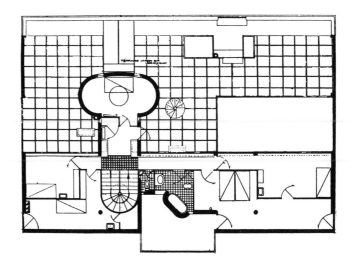

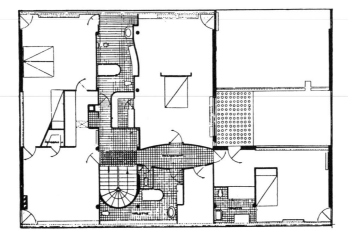

need hardly be assigned a source:

There was a great king with a young wife whom he loved to distraction. She died. He gathered the finest craftsmen in the world to build a beautiful sarcophagus for her, and he placed it in the center of his biggest mosque. Soon the architectural setting came to seem unworthy of the sarcophagus and its contents, and the king had the mosque rebuilt, larger, finer, grander, more splendid than before. He studied it for years. It was still not right. He rebuilt it once more, distilling it to pure space and air, pure light, blue, white, and gold. Again he studied it, long and hard, this time for many years. Something was still wrong. Finally he knew what it was. He called his vizier to him and pointed to the sarcophagus and said, "Take that thing away."

around it at last. When this process, a passionate and many-layered one, was complete, it had involved the most difficult but often most essential of creative acts, which is the elimination of the very heart of the original intention as the work of art grows. The story has been told so often that it

Venturi's abandonment of what could not conceivably be abandoned was less terrible, perhaps, but no less critical to him. And it was triple: he gave up, most of all, his very insignia, his conceit, the chimney, which was in large measure his self-love, and next the building blocks, and of course the ruins as deep layering, which, however, he most brilliantly incorporated, along with everything else, into the magisterial facade, which may have owed something critical to Luanda and Salk. Whatever the case, it was the ancestor of all the layerings of planes in space that were to play an important part in Venturi's later work and became, in turn, obsessive in that of hundreds of other architects.

A host of afterthoughts, regrets, and nervous qualifications seem to come flooding in at the very last, with some tiny sketches of the massing (VI/85, p.168; VI/87, p.170; VI/101, p.184). Most touching is a lovely, spare line drawing of the facade partly effaced by a heavy sketch of what may be a study for the fenestration of the living room but which looks for all the world like the Villa Savoye (VI/90, p.173). Where really can the truth be said to lie (the pun creates itself) and how can it be wholly told? Memories are treacherous in the oceanic flux of such endeavors, and words are another medium yet, reaching out with difficulty to translate the visual myth and evoke the material surface of the dream, most of all, of the mysterious physical process itself. But the words are there, most especially Kahn's as he asks in the drafting room what the building "wants to be," perhaps only vaguely guessing himself what he may mean.

Therefore, Venturi often brought his drawings for the Vanna Venturi House to Kahn's office after he had left Kahn's employ. Colleagues apparently made some models for him, and their memory, perhaps faulty, is that Kahn didn't seem to like the scheme very much. Perhaps he couldn't bring himself to do so or to tell them that he did. Others remember him as advising Vanna Venturi to go ahead and build. At any rate, Venturi was clearly doing things that were constitutionally unsympathetic to Kahn. Yet he had without question already learned a lot from Venturi, who, trained as he had been by the last indomitable corporal's guard of the French Beaux-Arts at Princeton, had never been subjected to the Germanic iconoclasm of modernism's most intolerant and limiting school—to which Kahn, at least in his professional life during the 1930s and '40s, had most destructively been exposed.

So Kahn himself was eventually liberated by Venturi to recall his own past, no less than that of humanity as a whole, and to build upon it. Those elements of design, mostly Roman, which are early in Venturi and late in Kahn, attest to that. Kahn, on the other hand, presented the young architect with a number of specific forms, most especially that diagonal in plan which he himself was almost never to use. But the relationship was much deeper, more painful, and much more important than that. Kahn indeed gave Venturi everything, a bit as Louis Sullivan had given the young Frank Lloyd Wright so long before, by engaging the younger man in his own grim struggle to define himself and to be. And Venturi, alone of all the fine architects who worked with Kahn and learned from him, accepted that challenge wholly, even if it had to mean, as it always seems to, the loss of the master's dearly desired love at last. So Venturi broke through, but alone, to an enhanced identity and another land. So Jacob wrestled with the angel at the passage of Penuel, who said to him:

"Let me go, for the day breaketh."

And he said, "I will not let thee go, except thou bless me."

And he said, "Thy name shall be called no more Jacob, but Israel: for as a prince thou hast power with God and with men, and hath prevailed."

New Haven, 1991

ILLUSTRATIONS

1. Le Corbusier. Villa Stein, Garches, near Paris, France, 1927–28, front facade, photo courtesy of The Museum of Modern Art, New York

2. Leonardo da Vinci, *Man of Perfect Proportions*, drawing, circa 1510

3. Kallman, McKinnell and Knowles, City Hall, Boston, Massachusetts, 1962–69, photo courtesy of Yale University

4. Philip Johnson, Glass House, New Canaan, Conneticut, 1949, photo by Alexandre Georges, courtesy of Philip Johnson

5. Robert Venturi, Beach House project, 1959, front elevation, courtesy of Venturi, Scott Brown and Associates

6. McKim, Mead and White, Low House, Bristol, Rhode Island, 1887, front elevation, photo by Wayne Andrews, from Vincent Scully, *The Shingle Style and the Stick Style*, 1971 (revised edition), courtesy of Yale University

7. Sir Edwin Lutyens, Middlefield, Great Shelford, Cambridgeshire, England, 1908, from A. S. G. Butler, *The Architecture of Sir Edwin Lutyens, Volume One*, 1950

8. Le Corbusier, Villa Savoye, Poissy, France, 1929–31, photo from Le Corbusier and Pierre Jeanneret, *Oeuvre Complète*, 1924–34

9. Frank Lloyd Wright, Wright House, Oak Park, Illinois, 1889, front facade, photo courtesy of Yale University

10. Louis I. Kahn, Goldenberg House project, Rydal, Pennsylvania, 1959, plan, by permission of the Louis I. Kahn Collection, University of Pennsylvania and Pennsylvania Historical and Museum Commission

11. Louis I. Kahn, Esherick House, Chestnut Hill, Philadelphia, Pennsylvania, 1959–61, front view, photo by Denise Scott Brown

12. Robert Venturi, Beach House project, 1959, front elevation, model, courtesy of Venturi, Scott Brown and Associates

13. Louis I. Kahn, U. S. Consulate project, Luanda, Angola, 1959–62, isometric detail of wall and roof detail, by permission of the Louis I. Kahn Collection, University of Pennsylvania and Pennsylvania Historical and Museum Commission

14. Louis I. Kahn, meeting house, Salk Institute for Biological Studies, La Jolla, California, 1959–65, detail of perspective, by permission of the Louis I. Kahn Collection, University of Pennsylvania and Pennsylvania Historical and Museum Commission

15. Armando Brasini, Forestry Building, E. U. R., Rome, Italy, 1940–42, plan, from Luca Brasini, *L'Opera Architettonica e Urbanistica di Armando Brasini*, 1979

16. Robert Venturi, Pearson House project, Chestnut Hill, Philadelphia, Pennsylvania, 1957, section, courtesy of Venturi, Scott Brown and Associates

17. Robert Venturi, Pearson House project, Chestnut Hill, Philadelphia, Pennsylvania, 1957, ground floor plan, courtesy of Venturi, Scott Brown and Associates

18. Louis I. Kahn, Fleischer House project, Elkins, Park, Pennsylvania, 1959, plan, by permission of the Louis I. Kahn Collection, University of Pennsylvania and Pennsylvania Historical and Museum Commission

19. Robert Venturi, Beach House project, 1959, ground floor plan, courtesy of Venturi, Scott Brown and Associates

20. Robert Venturi and William Short, Meiss House project, Princeton, New Jersey, 1962, ground floor plan, courtesy of Venturi, Scott Brown and Associates

21. Robert Venturi, Beach House project, 1959, section, courtesy of Venturi, Scott Brown and Associates

22. Robert Venturi, Beach House project, 1959, model, courtesy of Venturi, Scott Brown and Associates

23. Andrea Palladio, Villa Malcontenta, Foscari, Italy, circa 1560, rear elevation, photo by Frederic Schwartz

24. Louis I. Kahn, Fleischer House project, Elkins Park, Pennsylvania, 1959, model, photo by Marshall D. Meyers, by permission of the Louis I. Kahn Collection, University of Pennsylvania and Pennsylvania Historical and Museum Commission

25. Venturi and Rauch, Guild House, Philadelphia, Pennsylvania, 1960–63, front elevation, photo courtesy of Venturi, Scott Brown and Associates

26. Louis I. Kahn, U. S. Consulate project, Luanda, Angola, 1959–62, model, photo by John Condax, by permission of the Louis I. Kahn Collection, University of Pennsylvania and Pennsylvania Historical and Museum Commission

27. Louis I. Kahn, meeting house, Salk Institute for Biological Studies, La Jolla, California, 1959–65, model, by permission of the Louis I. Kahn Collection, University of Pennsylvania and Pennsylvania Historical and Museum Commission

28. Sir Edwin Lutyens, Witwood, Surrey, England, 1898, ground floor plan and east elevation, from A. S. G. Butler, *The Architecture of Sir Edwin Lutyens, Volume One,* 1950

29. Alvar Aalto, Cultural Center, Wolfsburg, Germany, 1959–63, ground floor plan

30. Sir Edwin Lutyens, Marvells, Sussex, England, 1911, ground floor plan, from A. S. G. Butler, *The Architecture of Sir Edwin Lutyens, Volume One,* 1950

31. Le Corbusier, Villa Stein, Garches, near Paris, France, 1927–28, second and third floor plans

FREDERIC SCHWARTZ

NOTES ON THE DRAWINGS

Robert Venturi loves to draw and he draws beautifully. The discovery of these drawings offers the unexpected pleasure of looking at his early, exquisite drafting technique, reflecting his ideas during a period of great critical thought. The majority of the drawings, published here for the first time, illustrate that he is a consummate architect, an inventive and skilled draftsman, and an artist of great skill. And, since there is no written record of the design process, they are our only source for study.

Most of the drawings are conventional plans, sections, and elevations, and they follow the accepted technical, stylistic, and material standards. So what makes them so special? It is Venturi's concern for detail and his gift of machinelike precision and masterly control of the line weight. The drawings bear his mark of a faint and delicate underlying layer of measured calculation lines superimposed by a confident and bold final outline. Like Frank Lloyd Wright, Venturi treats architectural drawings as a design tool, not as a precious artifact. Many of the drawings for the house exhibit in-progress notes, calculations, erasures, and changes.

The vast majority of the drawings are of lead on vellum paper, and drawn with a T-square and triangle; there are also a few of marker, pencil, and colored marker on blueprint paper. Venturi did not use ink—he considered it too final and only appropriate for more formal presentation drawings. Very few of the well-known sketches on yellow tracing paper—a part of his normal design process—were found, a fact that can be attributed to the presence of a nearby wastebasket during the early years of his career. The drawings here were made only for Venturi and his mother; the earlier ones were drawn at his mother's home and the later ones at his office.

Like Le Corbusier, Venturi believes that the plan is the generator of form. These drawings illustrate his idea that elevations and sections develop from tension in the plan created by differences between inside and outside requirements. In this house, Venturi constantly switched back and forth between drawings of plans, sections, and elevations, and, because of its complexity and layering, he spent a lot of time, he recalls, studying the building in section.

Venturi's students at the University of Pennsylvania made models of bass wood and cardboard of the various design alternatives, which were used to study the house and its layers in three dimensions. As working models, they were rough and cut up, and although sometimes shown to his mother, they were not presentation models.

The twelve construction drawings of the house are of pencil on vellum, dated May 24, 1963, and sealed with Venturi's Pennsylvania

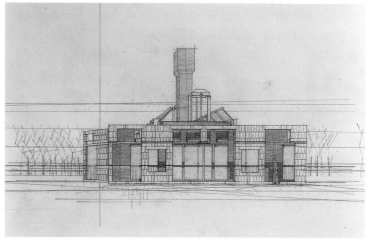

architect's stamp. The set was drafted primarily by Arthur Jones under the supervision of and with the assistance of Venturi and John Rauch.

Approximately thirty clarifying sketches (SKs) of details, lavishly noted and drawn by Venturi during construction of the house, illustrate his concern for detail and precision; thirty years later he can still be found at the drafting board suffering over the most minute detail. (A story circulated around Princeton during his student days that he could spend all day deciding on, and drafting, one line.)

All of the drawings are maintained in the office archives of Venturi, Scott Brown and Associates, with the exception of ten drawings that are in the collection of the Deutsches Architekturmuseum in Frankfurt, Germany, and three others, along with six study models, that are in the collection of The Museum of Modern Art in New York.

One hundred fourteen drawings, on the following pages, are identified by scheme and drawing number. At the end of the book, a complete listing of the drawings includes type, dimensions, medium, date of execution, and the firm's archival reference number.

SCHEME

I

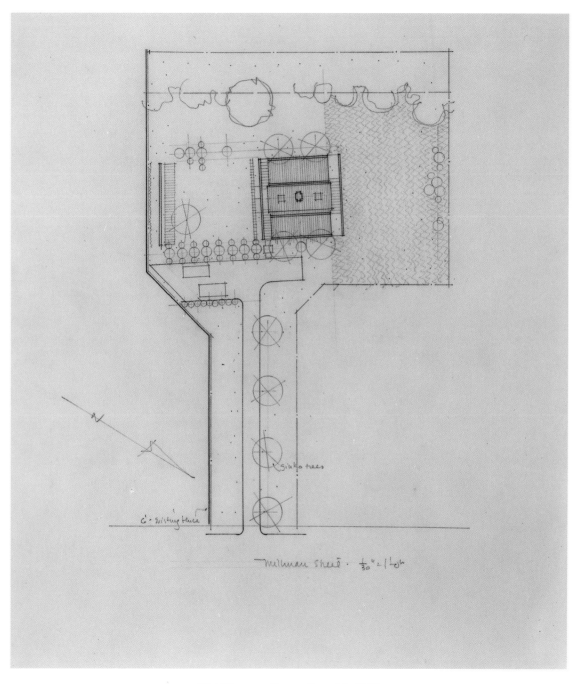

Plot Plan, pencil on vellum, July 1959

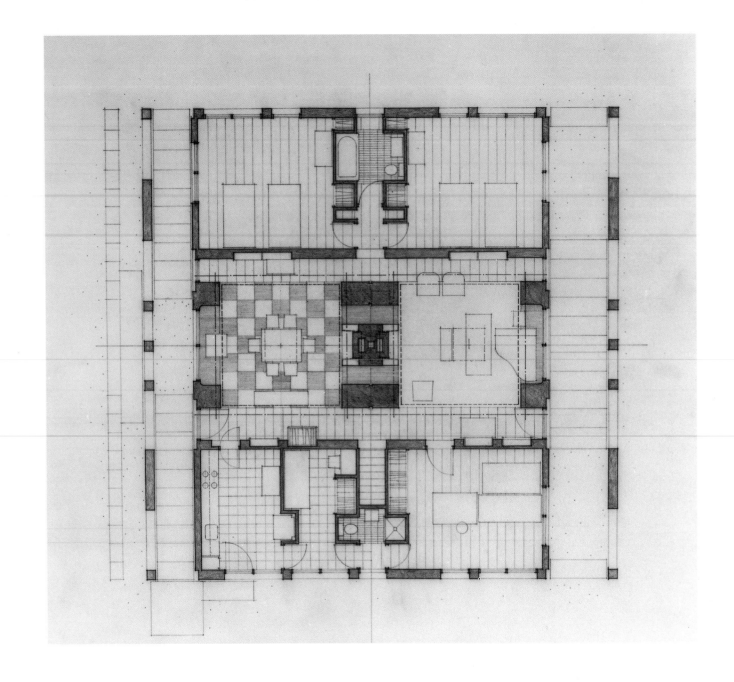

First Floor Plan, pencil and colored pencil on yellow trace, July 1959

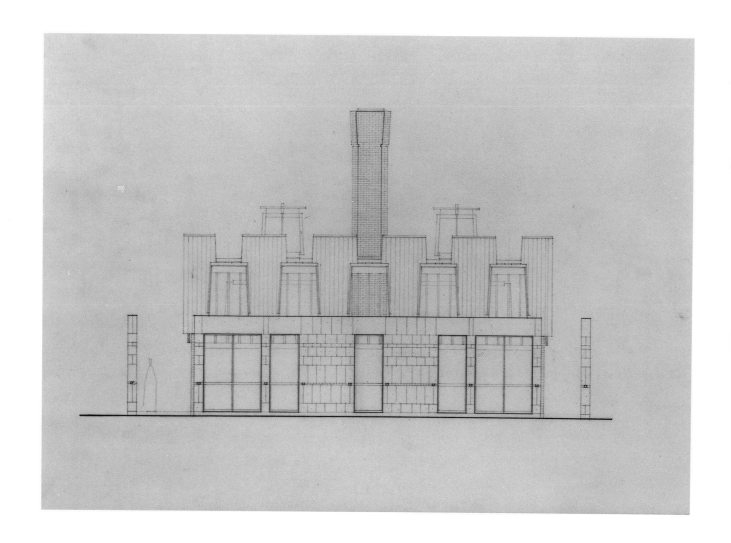

Rear Elevation, west, pencil on vellum, July 1959

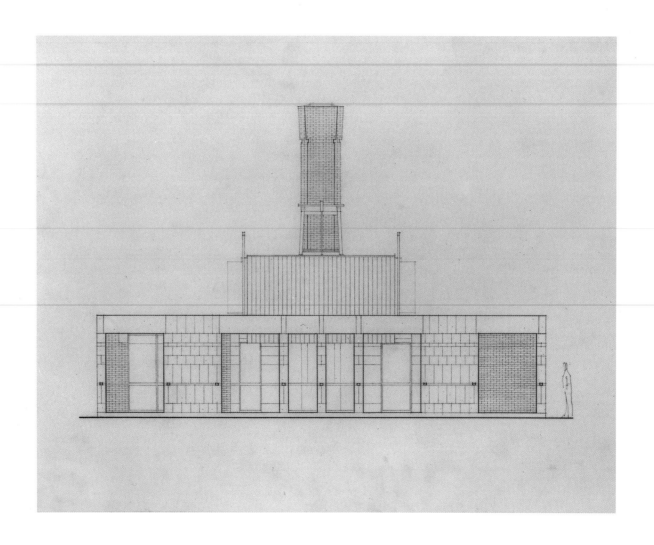

Side Elevation, south (with screen wall), pencil on vellum, July 1959

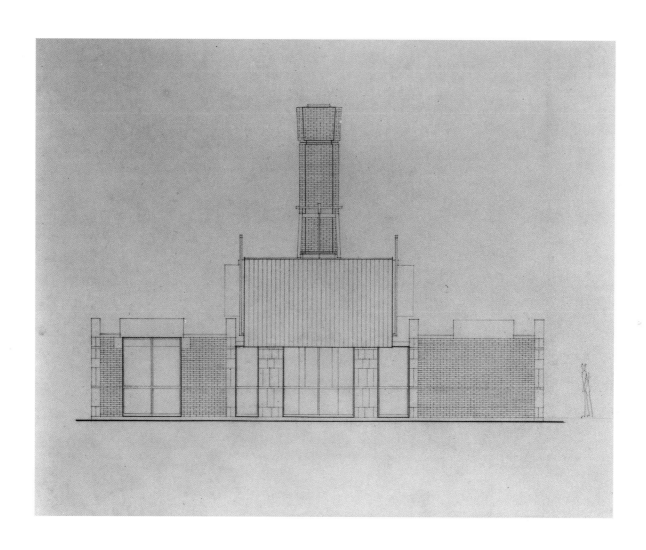

Side Elevation, south (without screen wall), pencil on vellum, July 1959

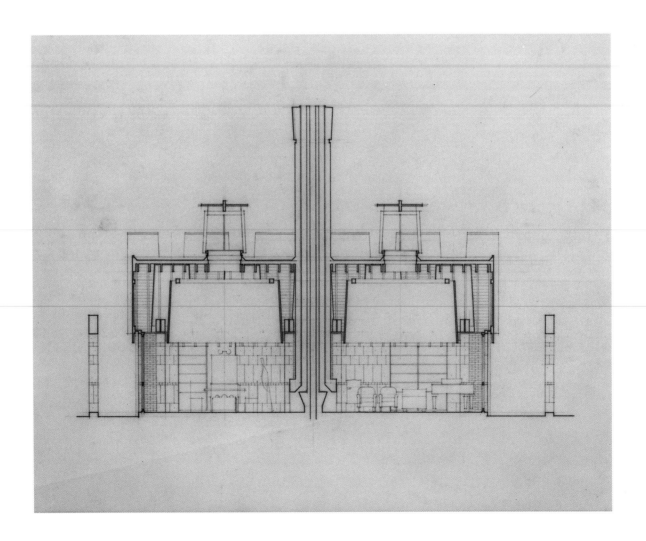

Section, pencil on vellum, July 1959

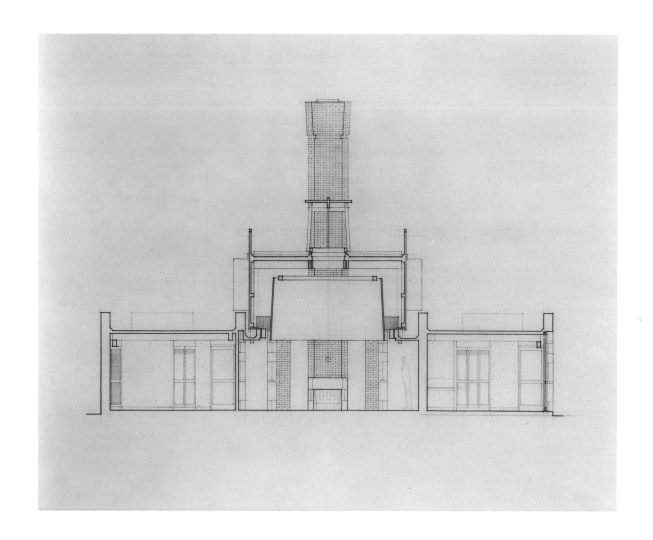

Section, pencil on vellum, July 1959

SCHEME

IIA

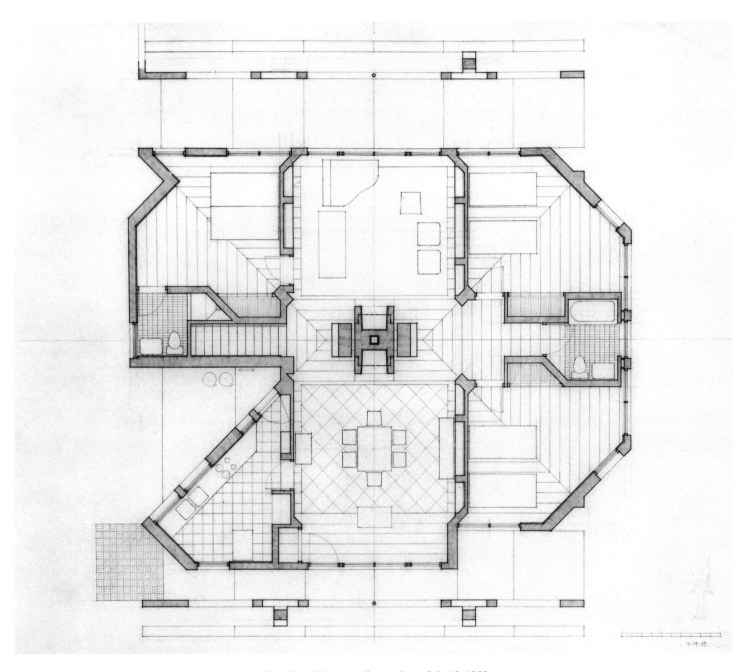

First Floor Plan, pencil on vellum, July 19, 1959

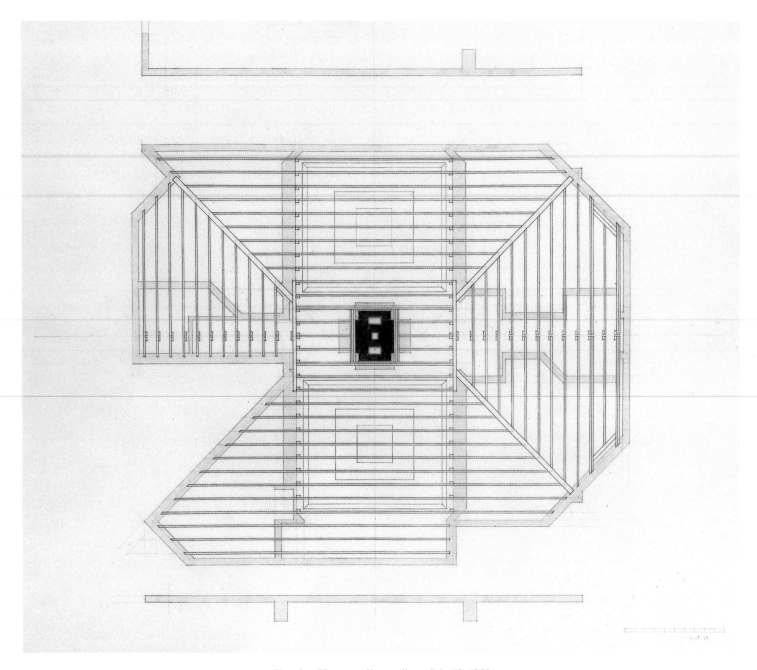

Framing Plan, pencil on vellum, July 19, 1959

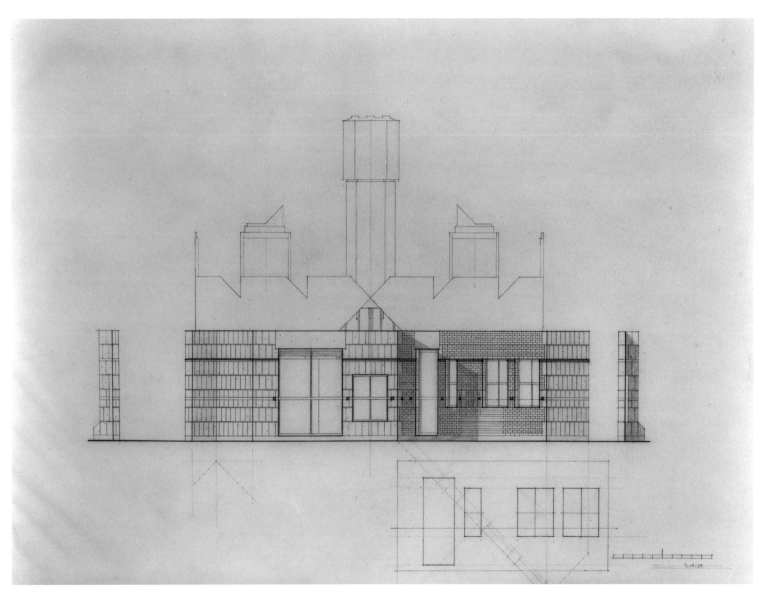

Front Elevation, east, pencil on vellum, July 19, 1959

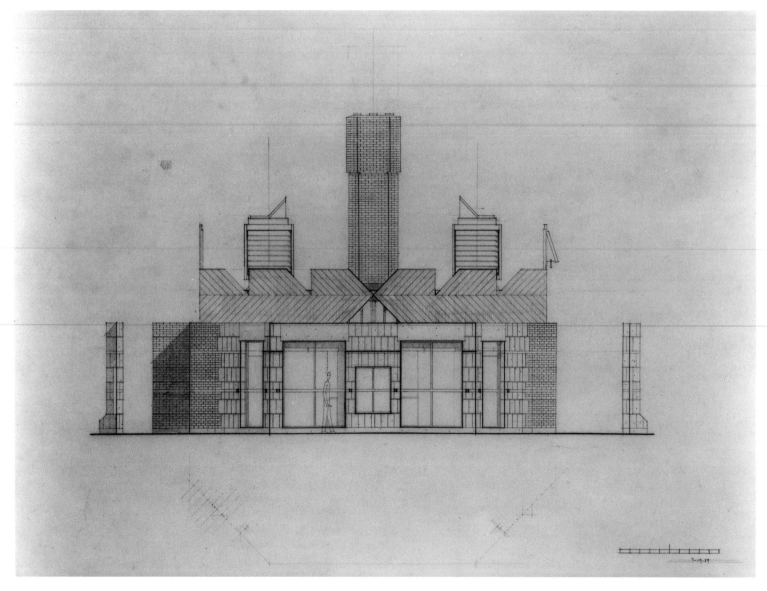

Rear Elevation, west, pencil on vellum, July 19, 1959

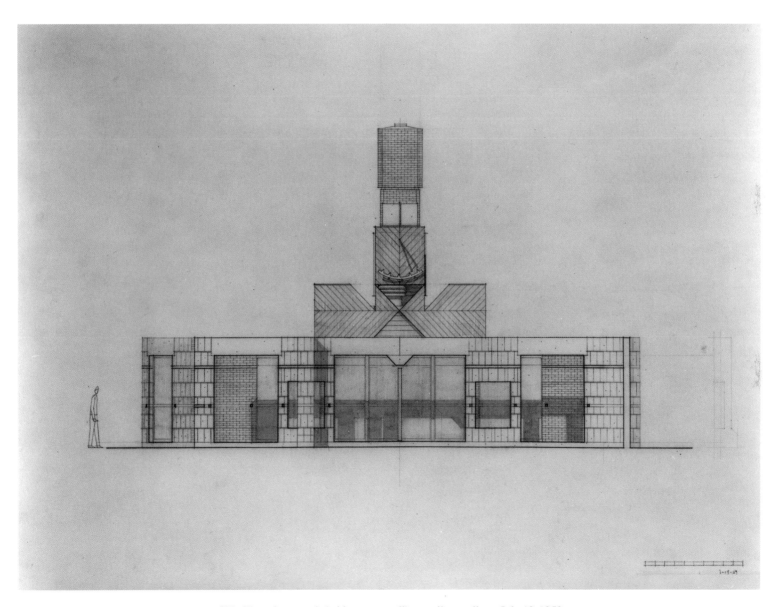

Side Elevation, south (with screen wall), pencil on vellum, July 19, 1959

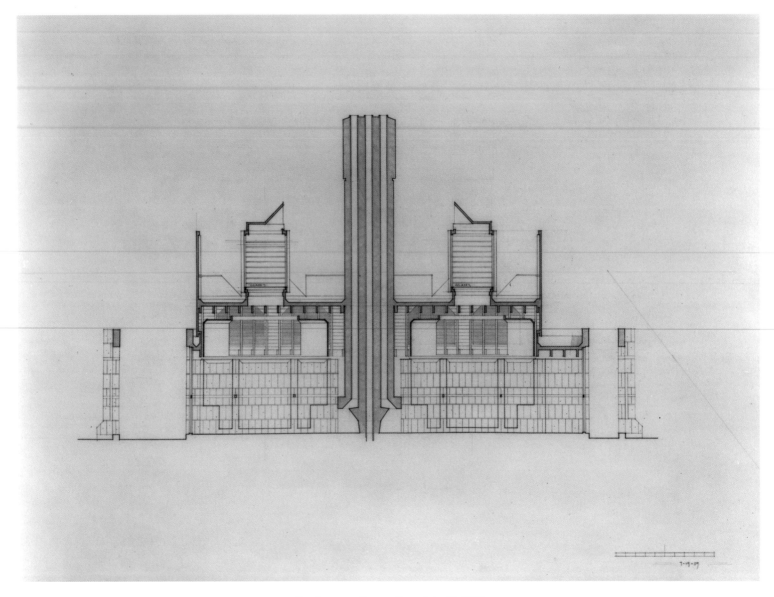

Section, pencil on vellum, July 19, 1959

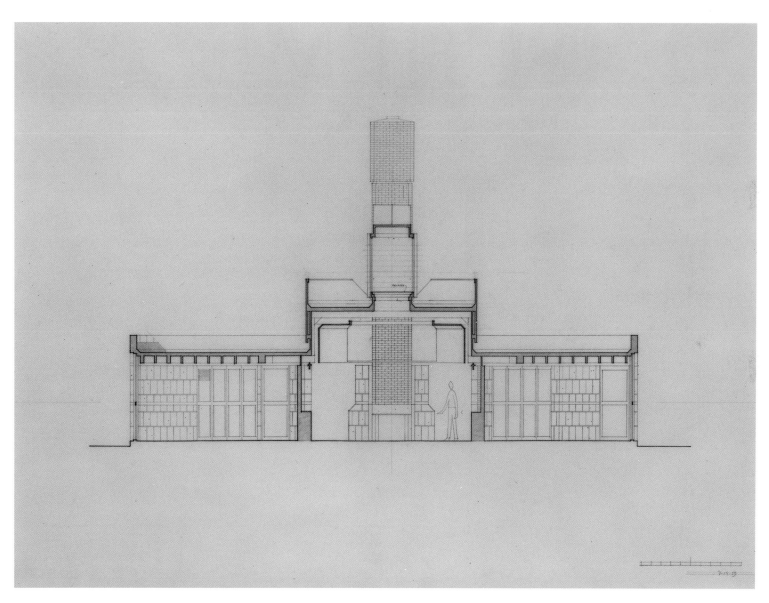

Section, pencil on vellum, July 19, 1959

SCHEME

IIB

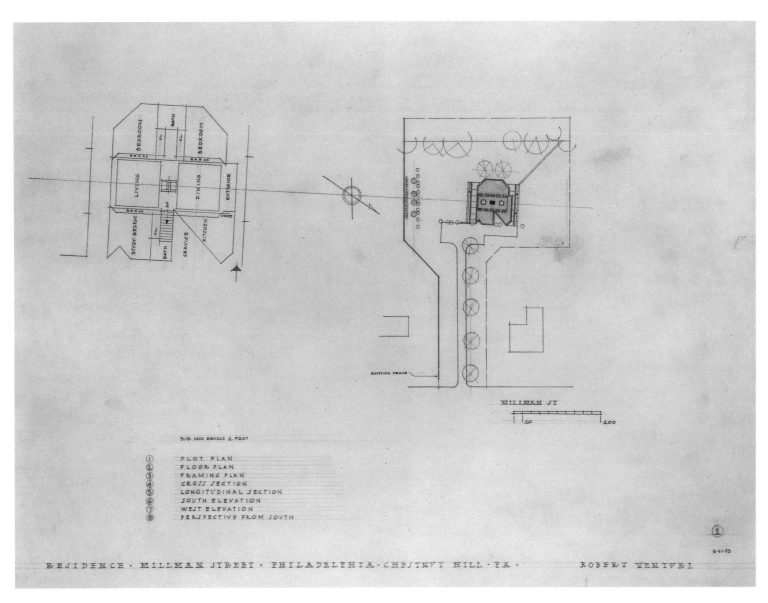

Plot Plan, pencil on vellum, August 31, 1959

First Floor Plan, pencil on vellum, August 31, 1959

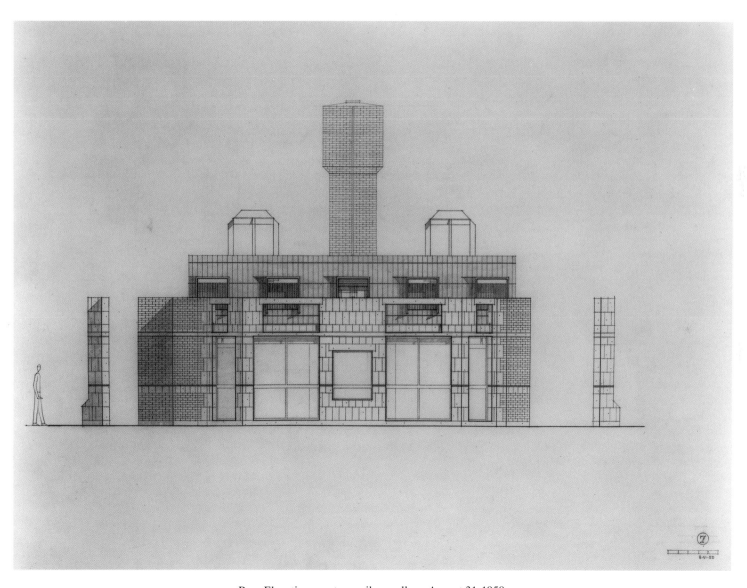

Rear Elevation, west, pencil on vellum, August 31, 1959

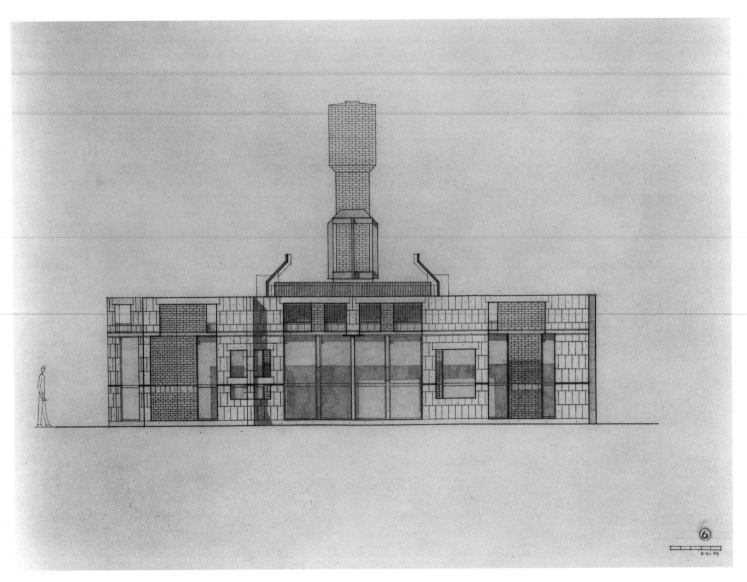

Side Elevation, south (with screen wall), pencil on vellum, August 31, 1959

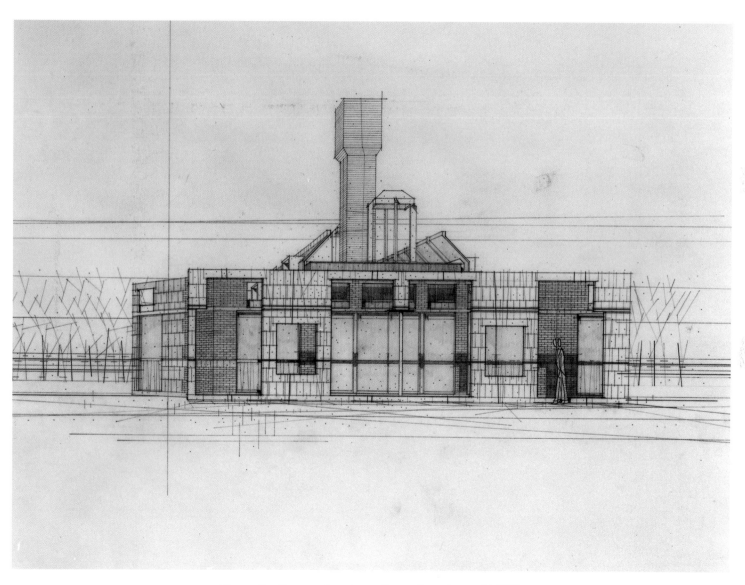

Perspective from southwest, pencil on vellum, August 31, 1959

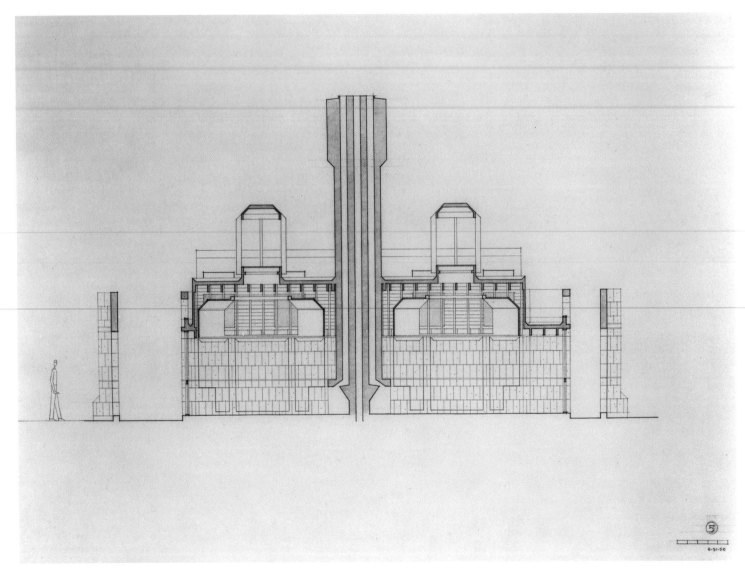

Section, pencil on vellum, July 1959

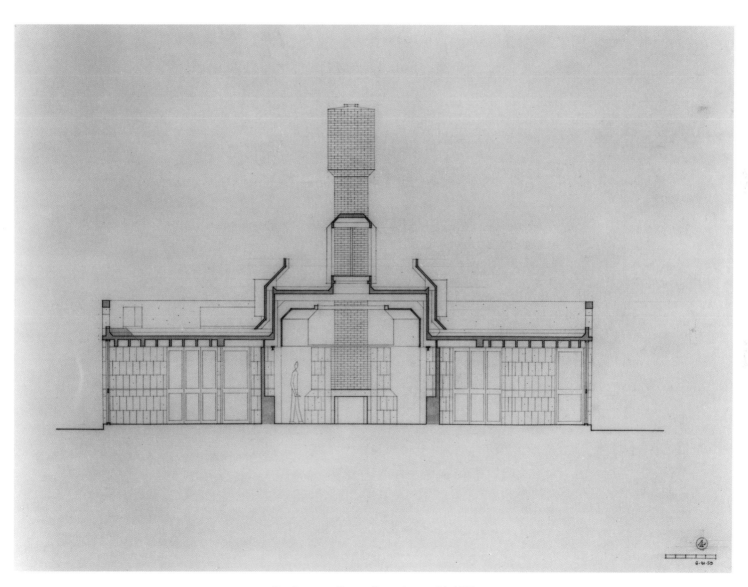

Section, pencil on vellum, August 31, 1959

SCHEME

IIC

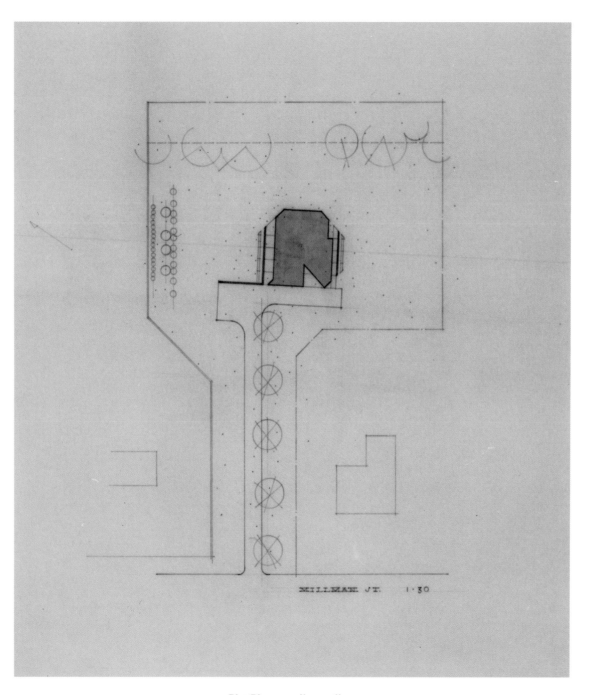

Plot Plan, pencil on vellum

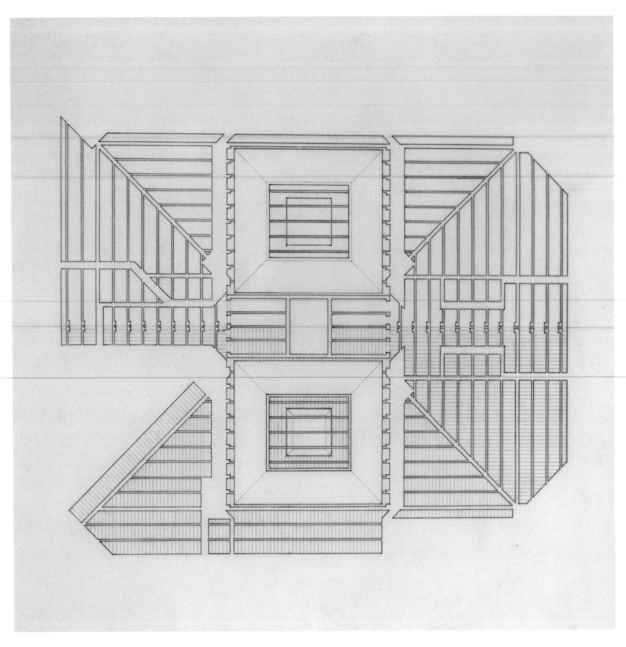

Roof framing plan, pencil on vellum

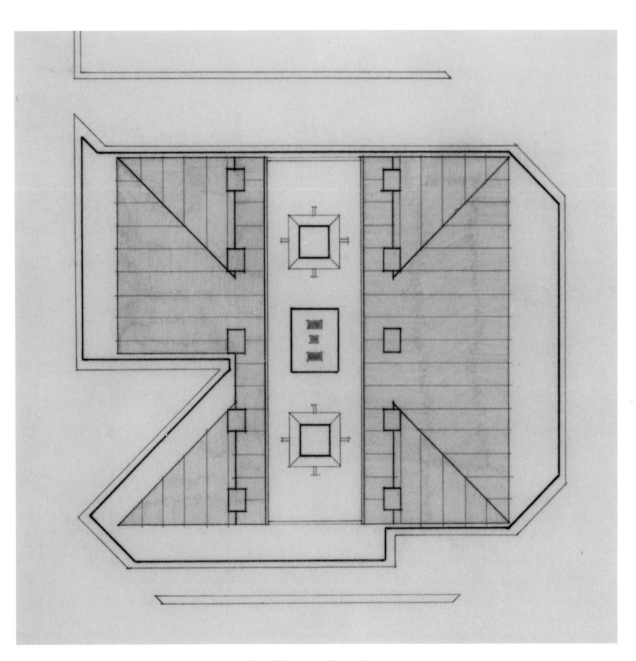

Roof Plan, pencil on vellum

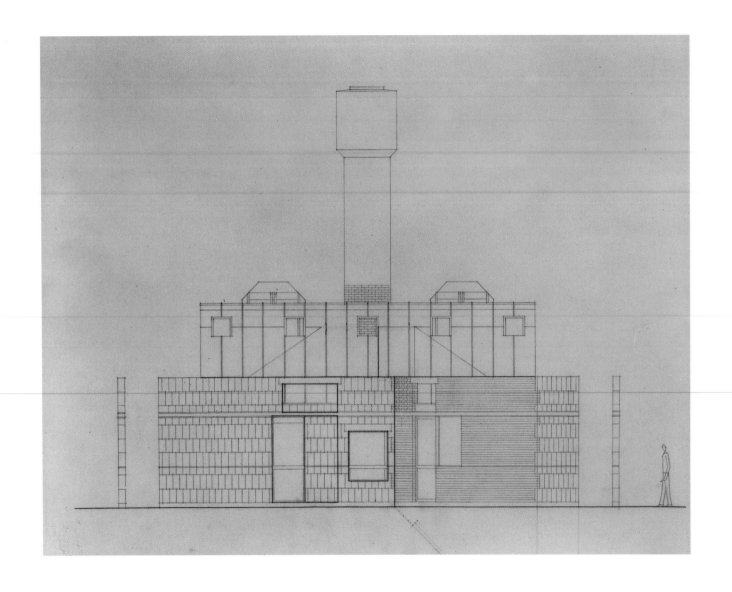

Front Elevation, east, pencil on vellum

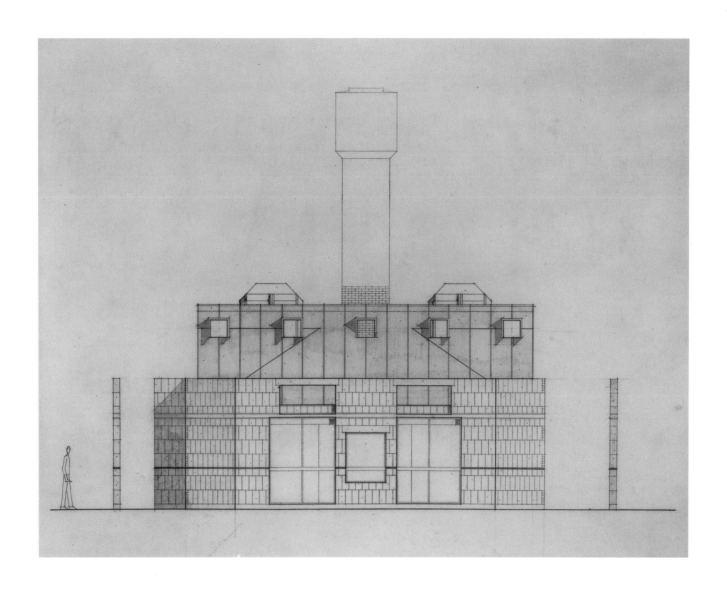

Rear Elevation, west, pencil on vellum

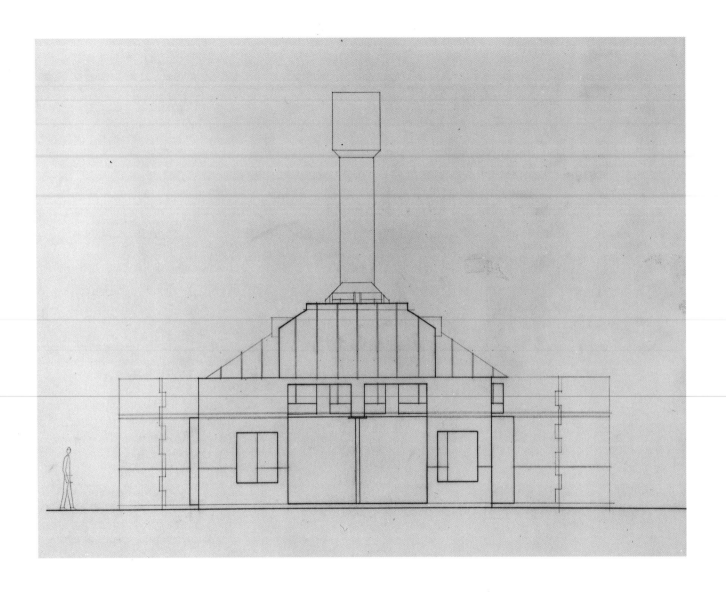

Side Elevation, north, study, pencil on vellum

Side Elevation, north, pencil on vellum

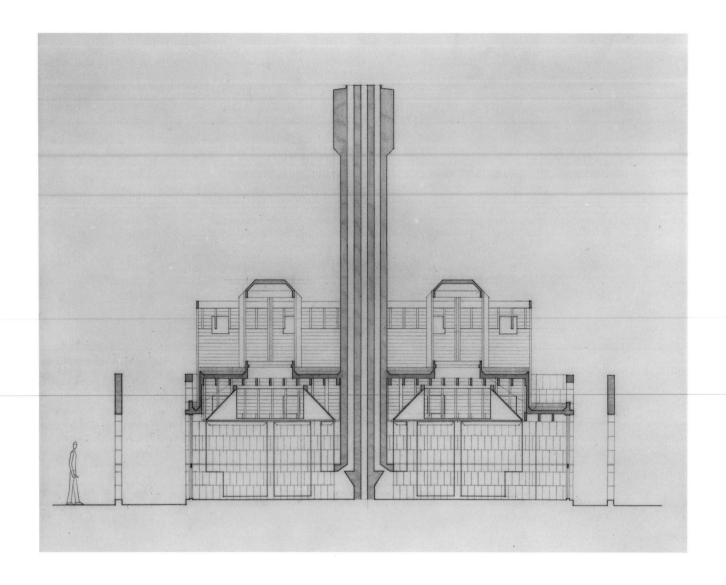

Section, pencil on vellum

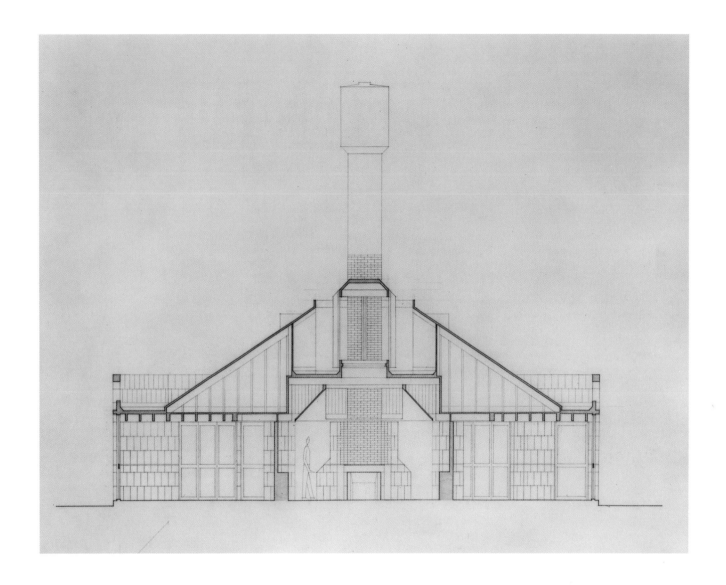

Section, pencil on vellum

SCHEME

IIIA

Model, chipboard and wood

Model, chipboard and wood

Model, chipboard and wood

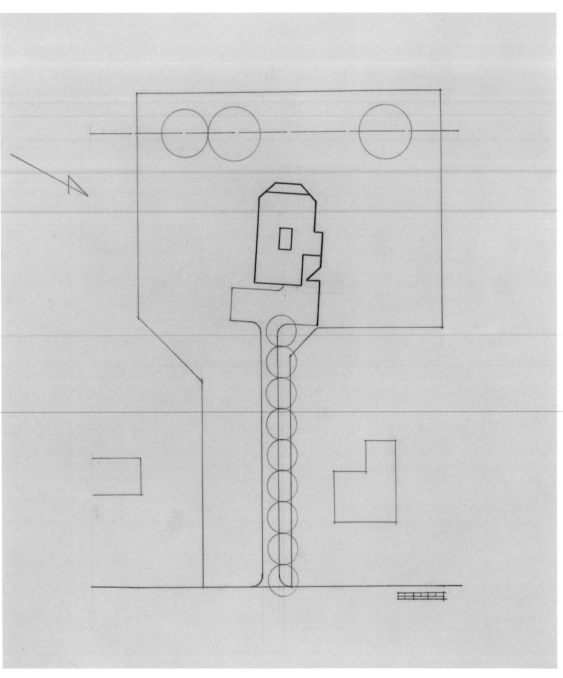

Plot Plan, pencil on vellum

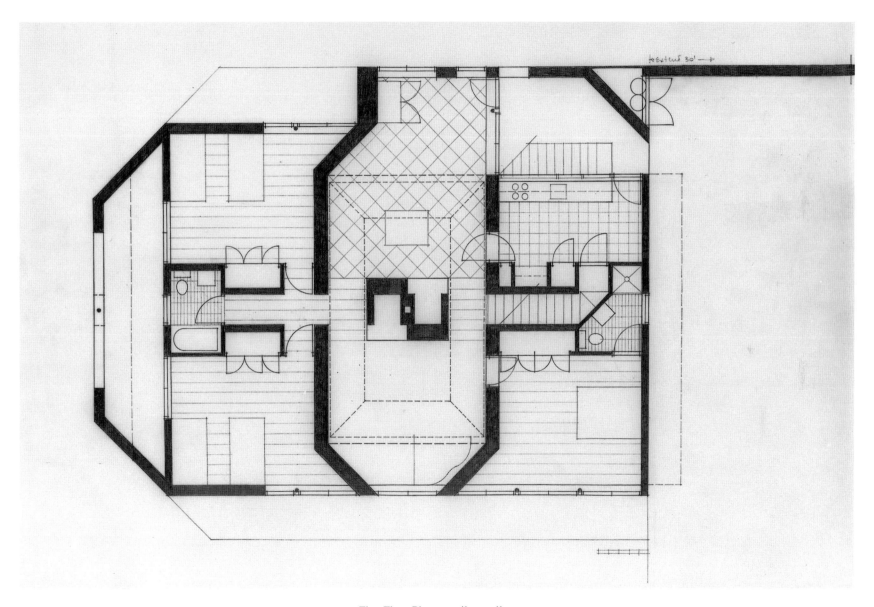

First Floor Plan, pencil on vellum

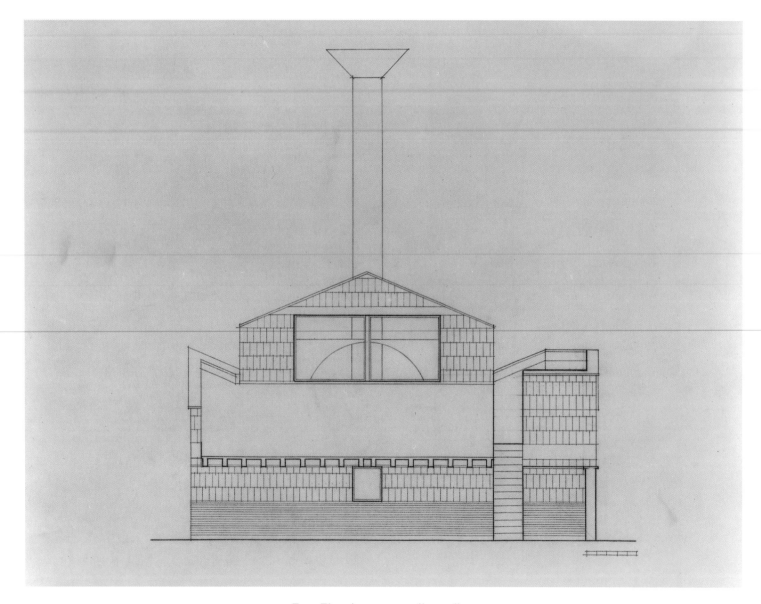

Front Elevation, east, pencil on vellum

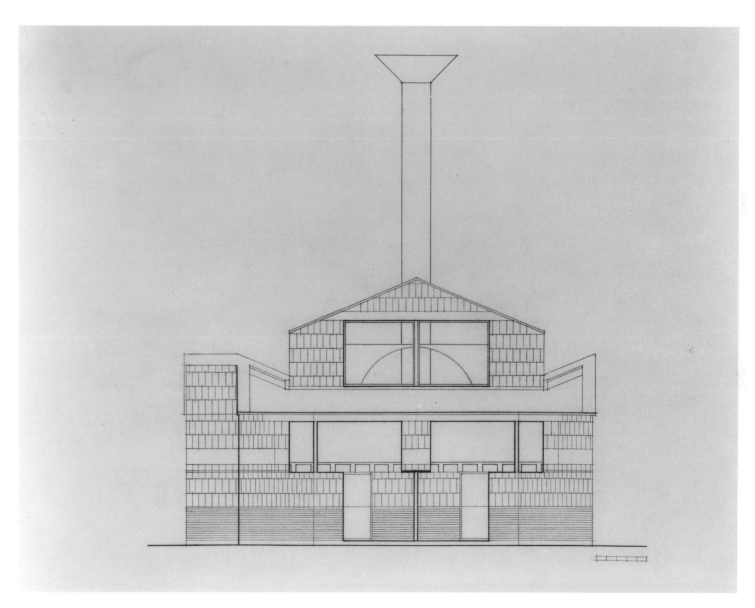

Front Elevation, east, pencil on vellum

Side Elevation, south, pencil on vellum

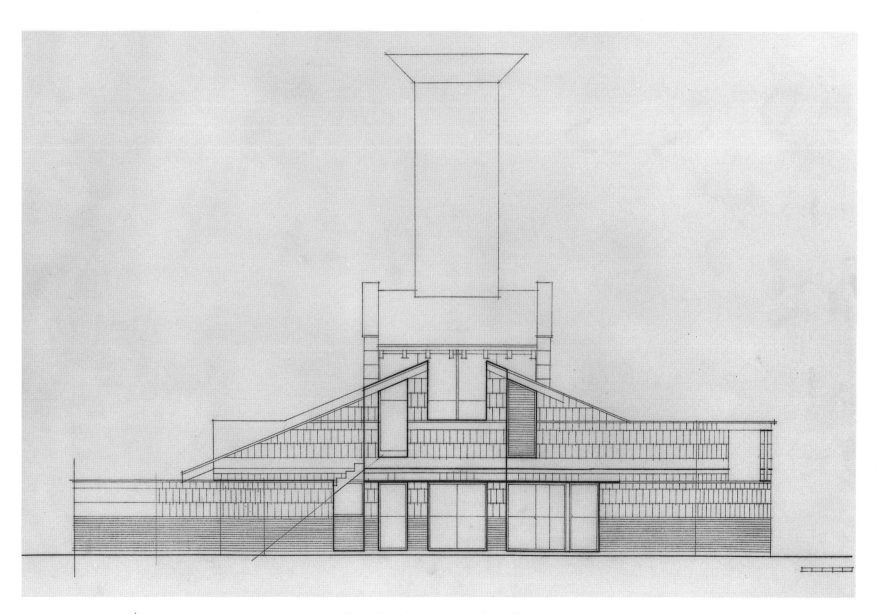

Front Elevation, north, pencil on vellum

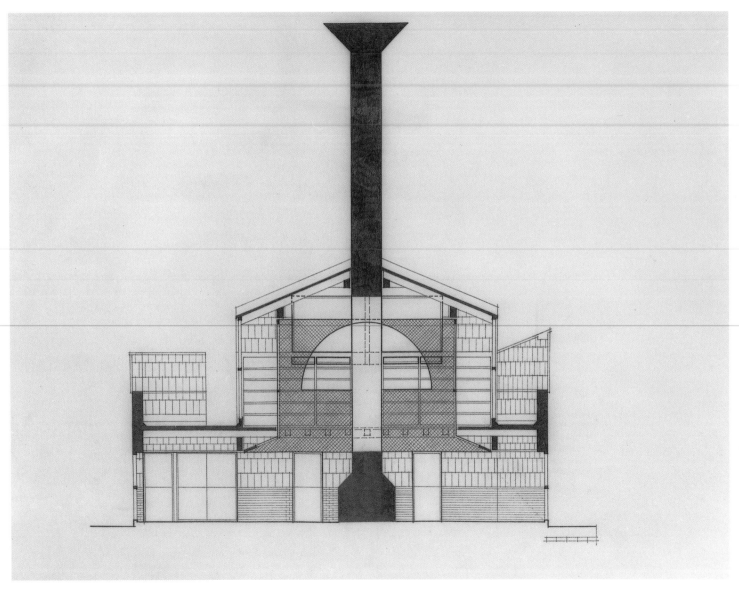

Section, pencil on vellum

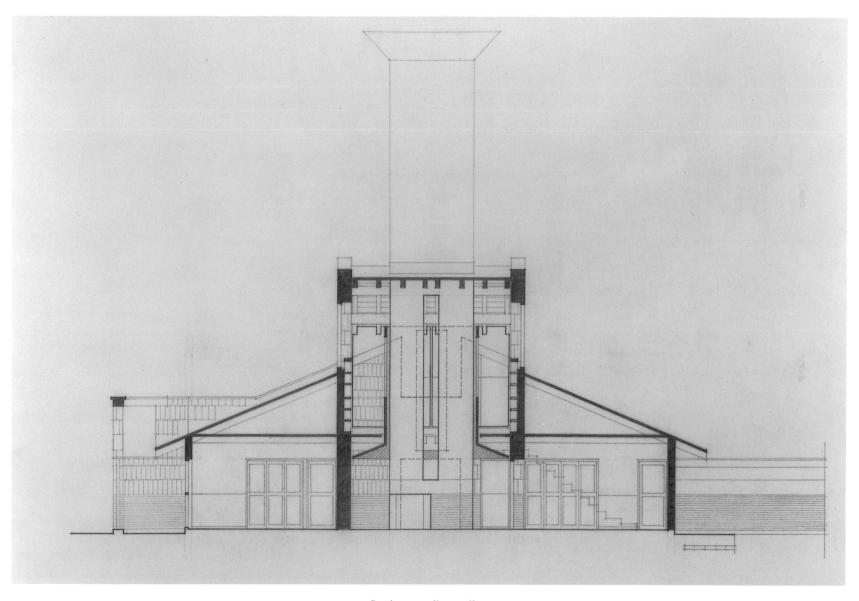

Section, pencil on vellum

SCHEME

IIIB

Model, chipboard and wood

Model, chipboard and wood

Model, chipboard and wood

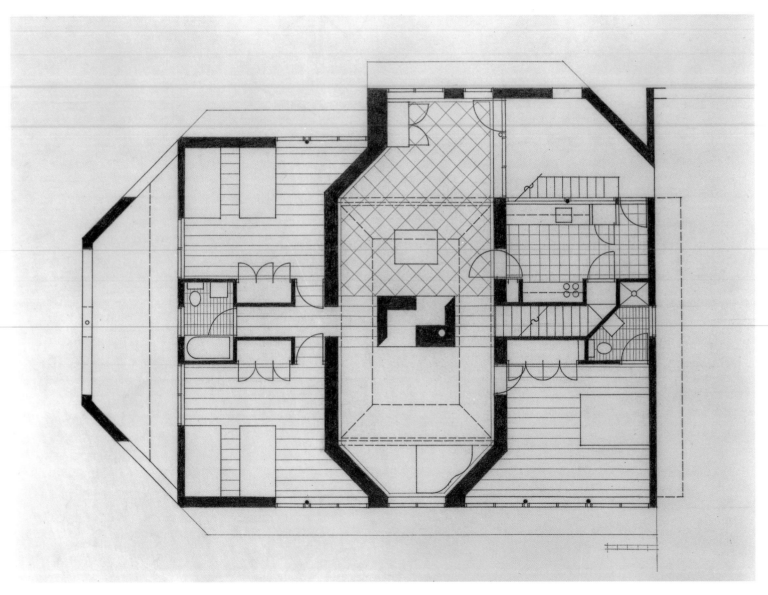

First floor plan, pencil on vellum

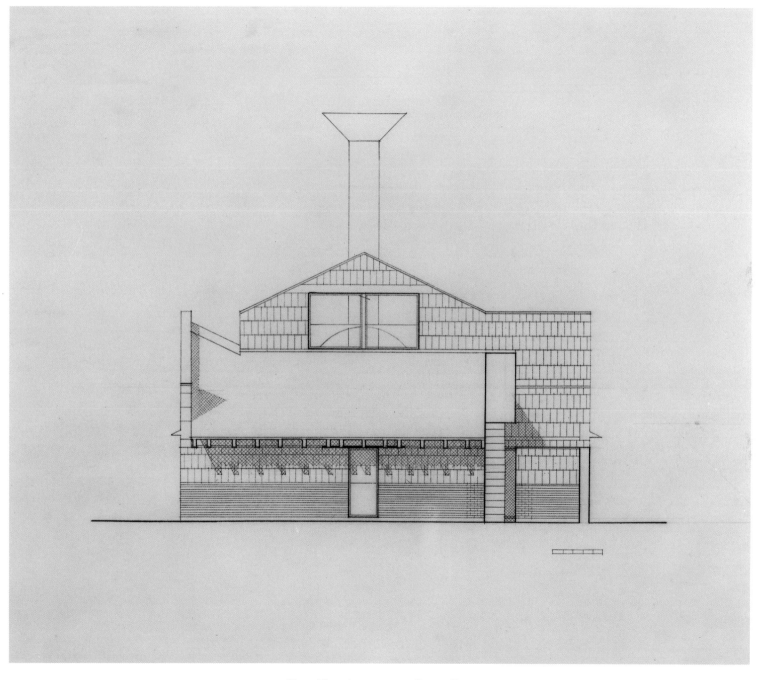

Front Elevation, east, pencil on vellum

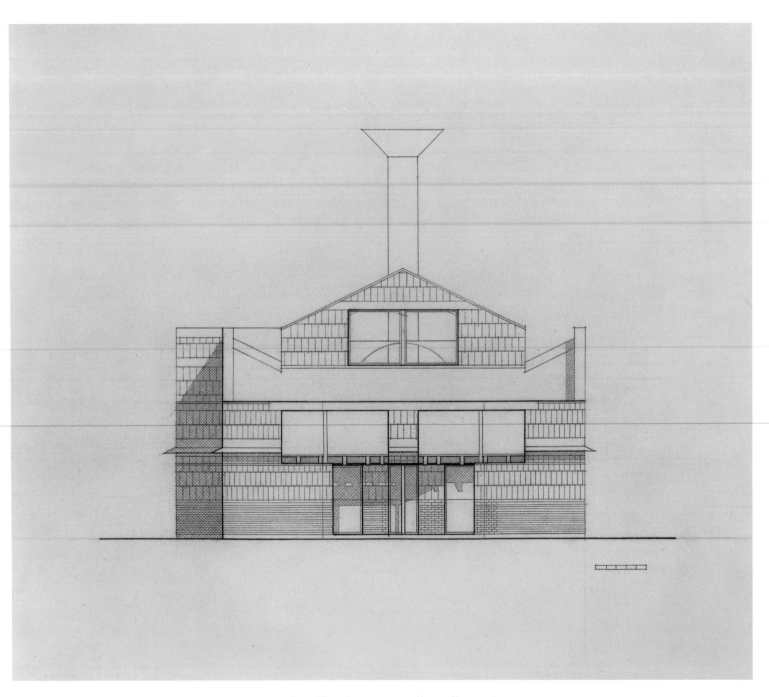

Rear Elevation, west, pencil on vellum

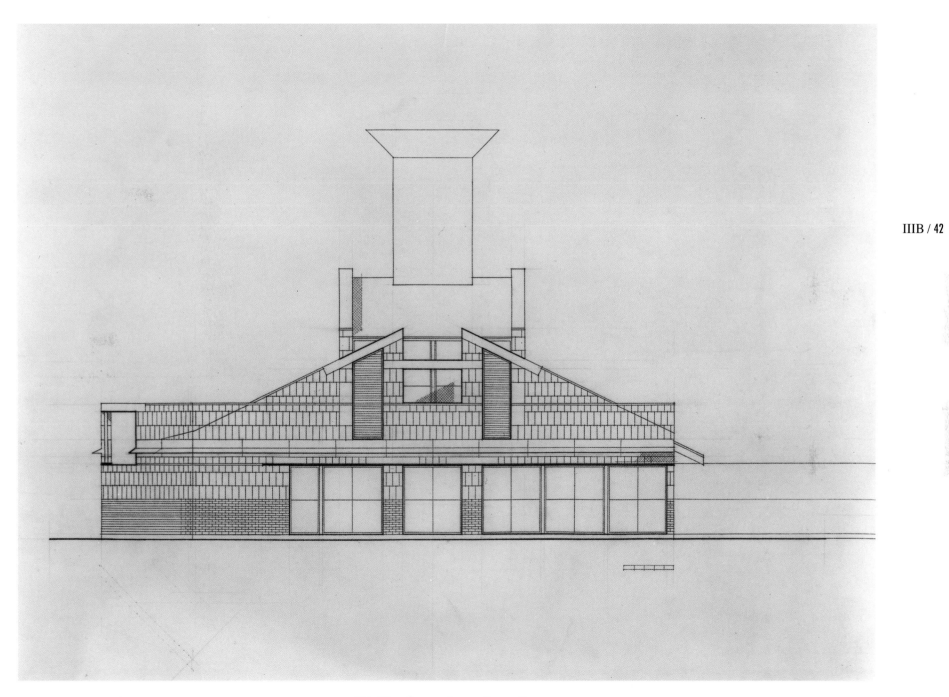

Side Elevation, south, pencil on vellum

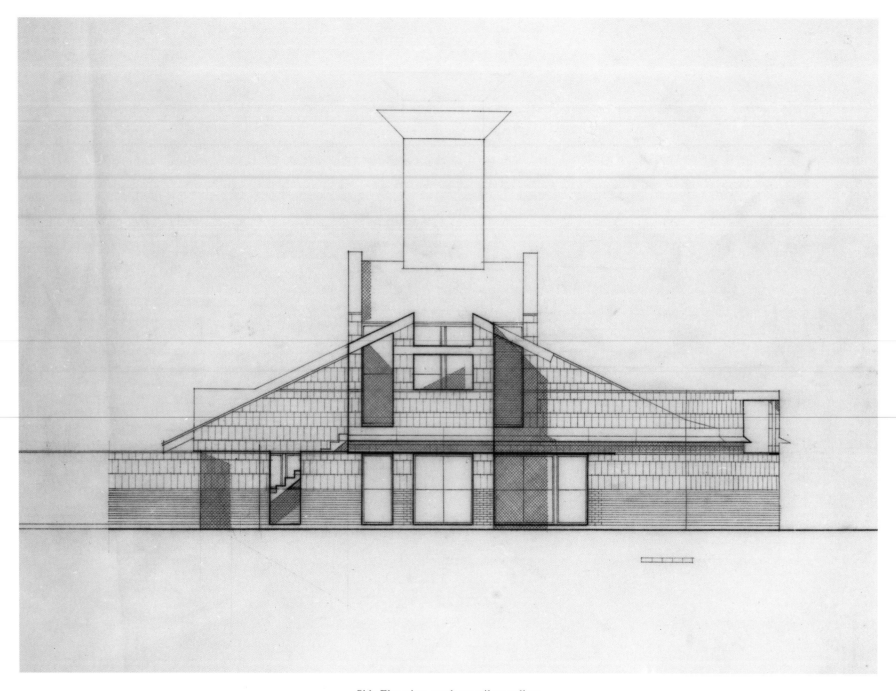

Side Elevation, north, pencil on vellum

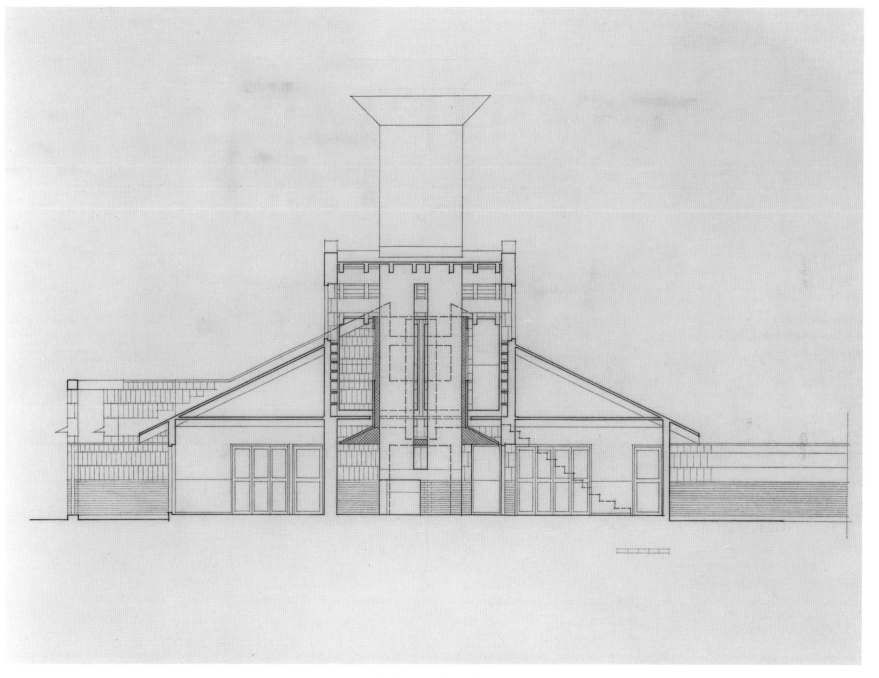

Section, pencil on vellum

SCHEME

IVA

Model, chipboard and wood

117.

Model, chipboard and wood

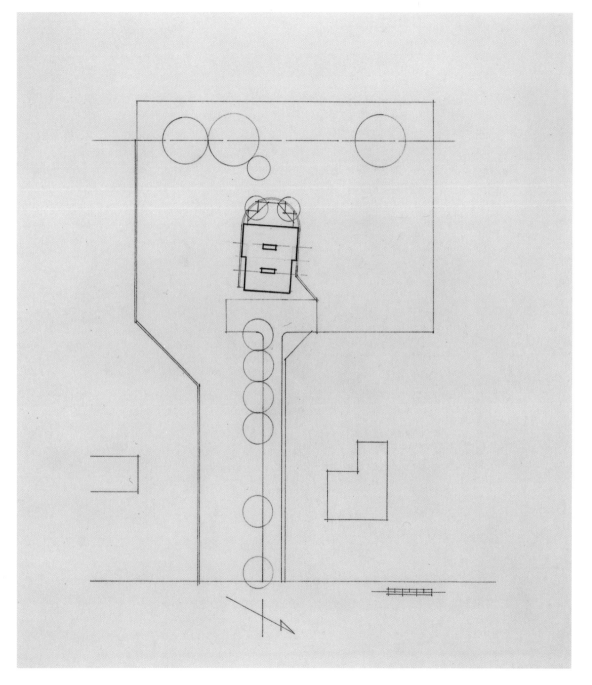

Plot Plan, pencil on vellum, July 12, 1961

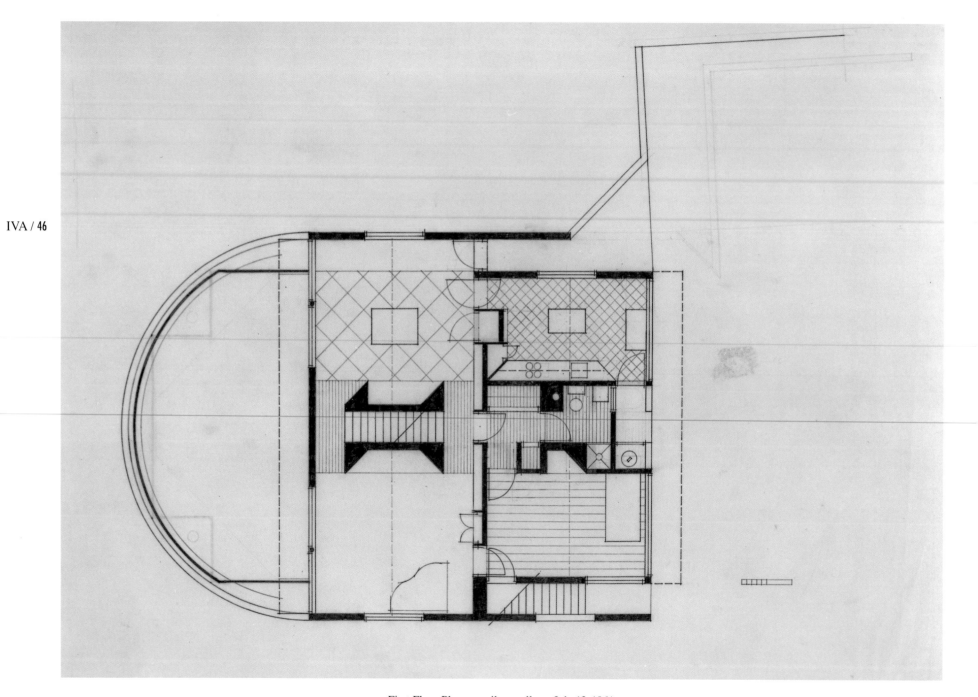

First Floor Plan, pencil on vellum, July 12, 1961

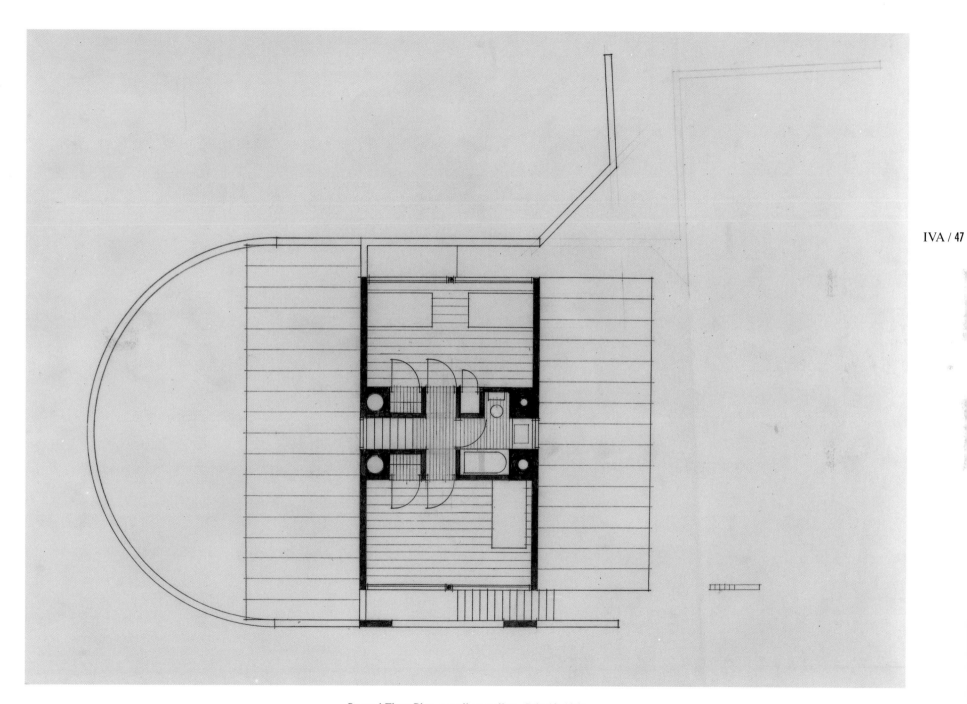

Second Floor Plan, pencil on vellum, July 12, 1961

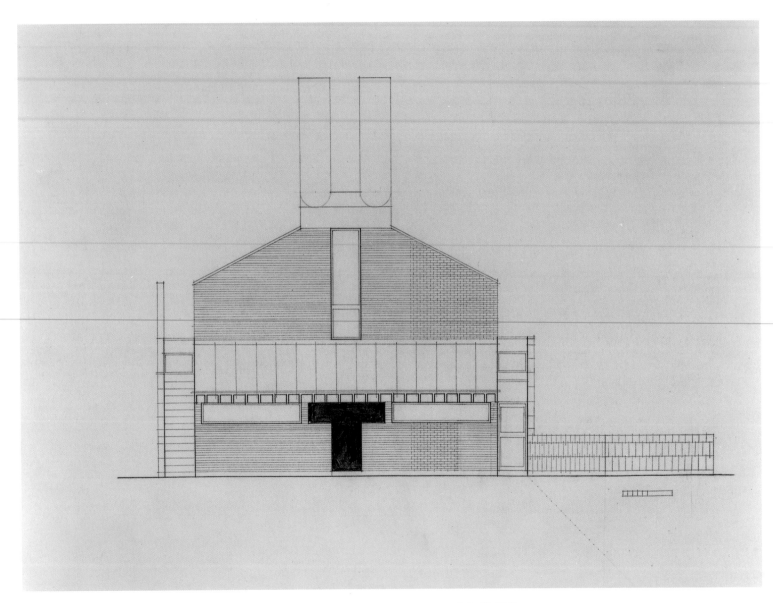

Front Elevation, east, pencil on vellum, July 12, 1961

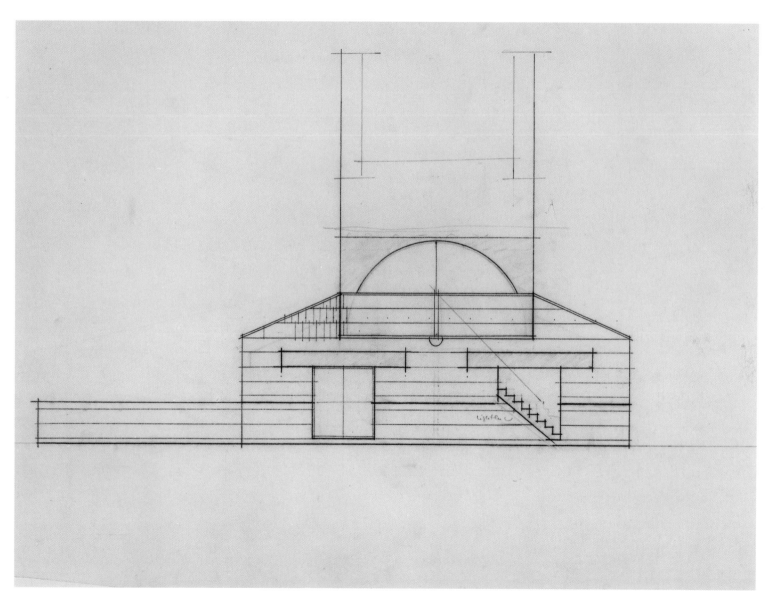

Side Elevation, south, study, pencil on vellum

Side Elevation, south, pencil on vellum, July 12, 1961

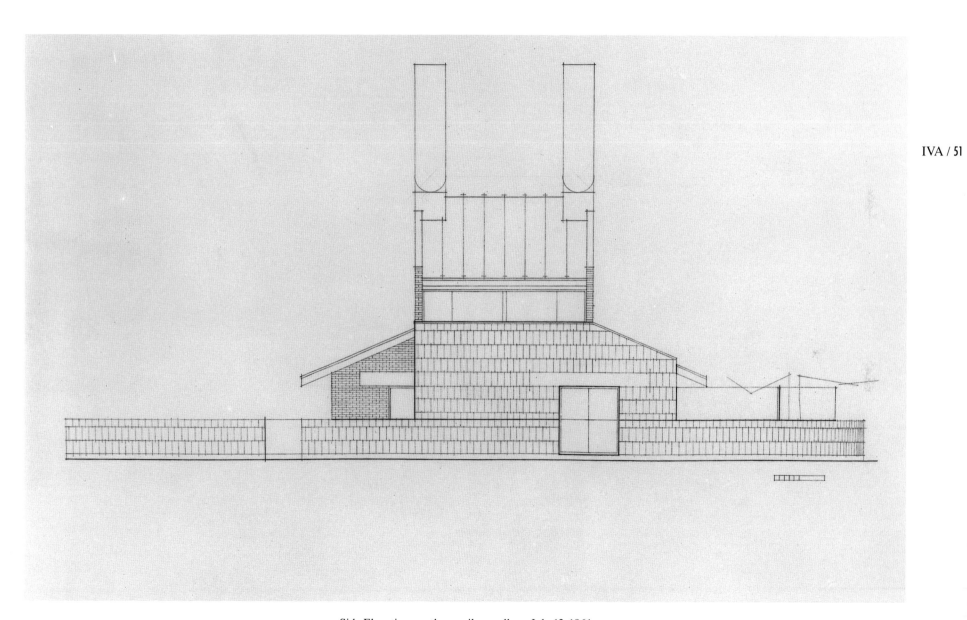

Side Elevation, north, pencil on vellum, July 12, 1961

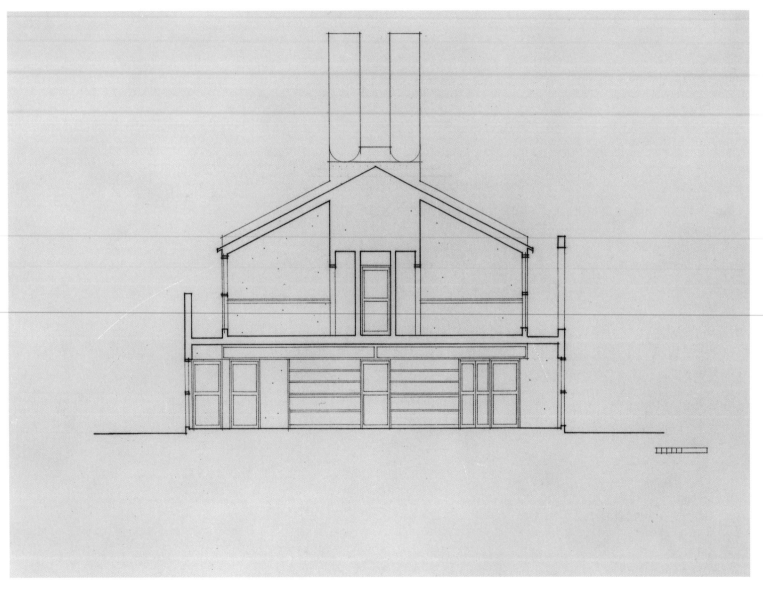

Section, pencil on vellum, July 12, 1961

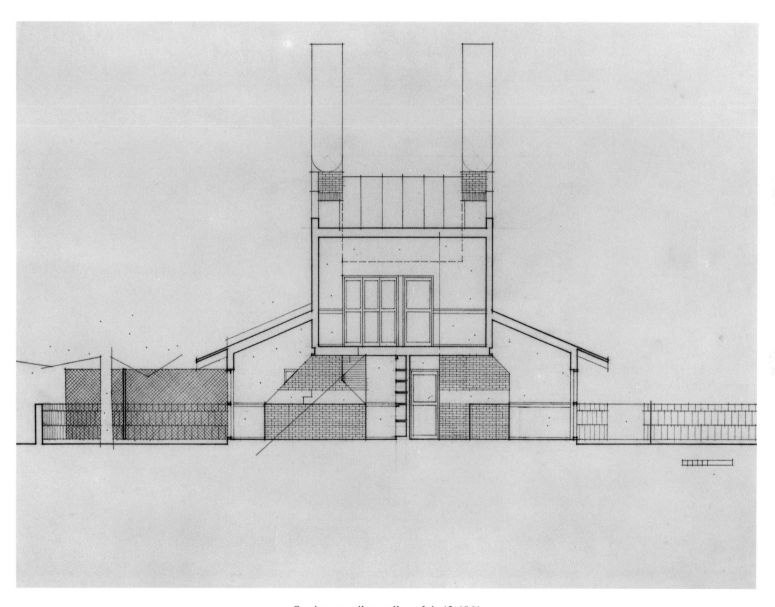

Section, pencil on vellum, July 12, 1961

SCHEME

IVB

Model, chipboard and cut paper

Model, chipboard and cut paper

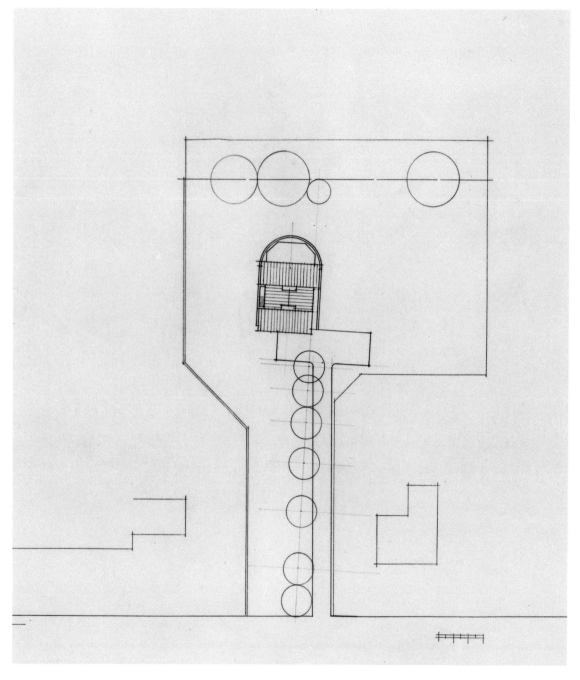

Plot Plan, pencil on vellum

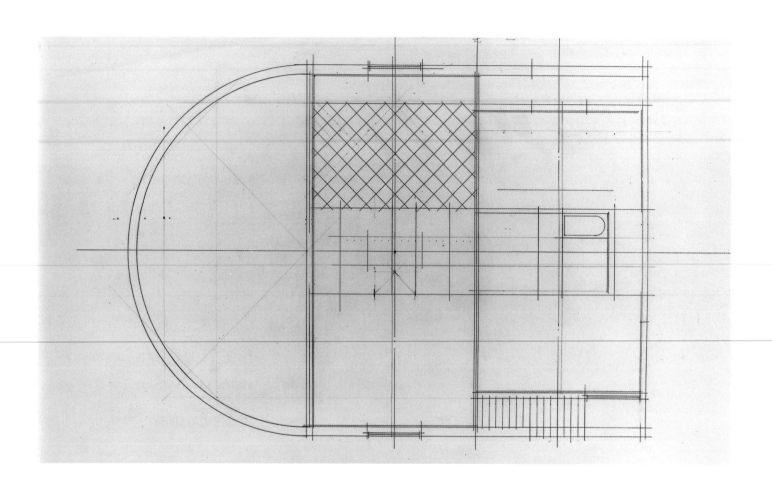

First Floor Plan, study, pencil on vellum

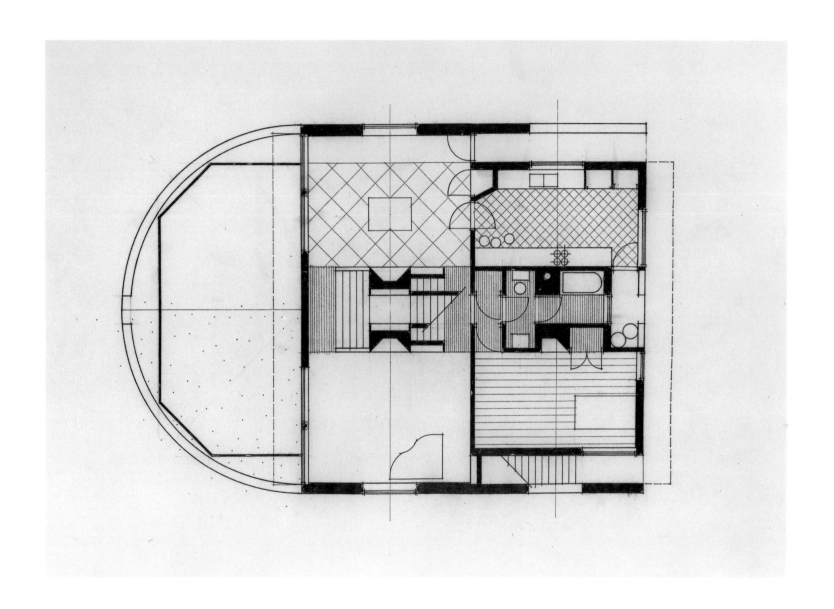

First Floor Plan, pencil on vellum

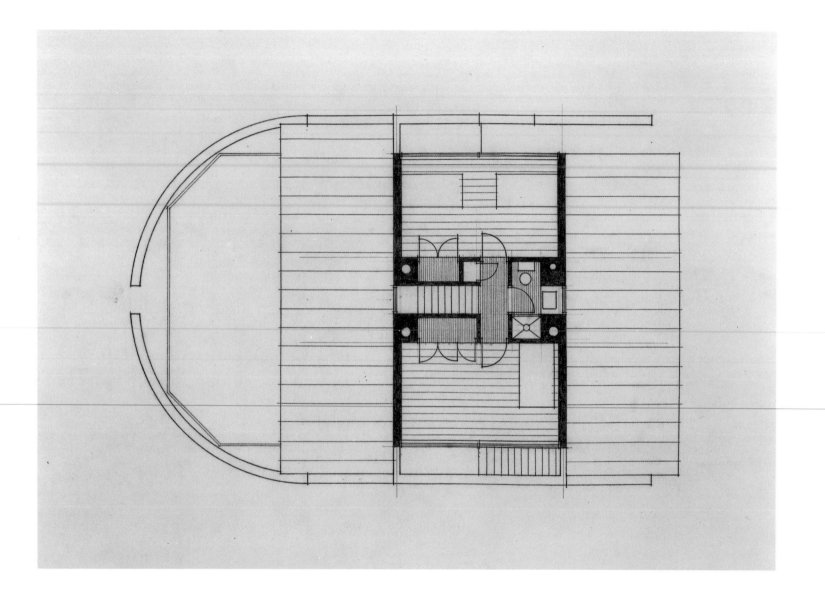

Second Floor Plan, pencil on vellum

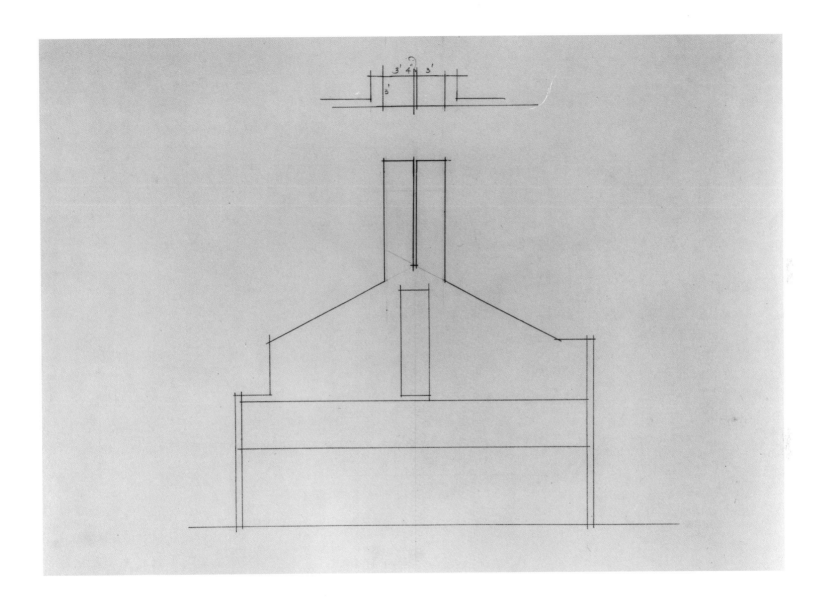

Front Elevation, east, study, pencil on vellum

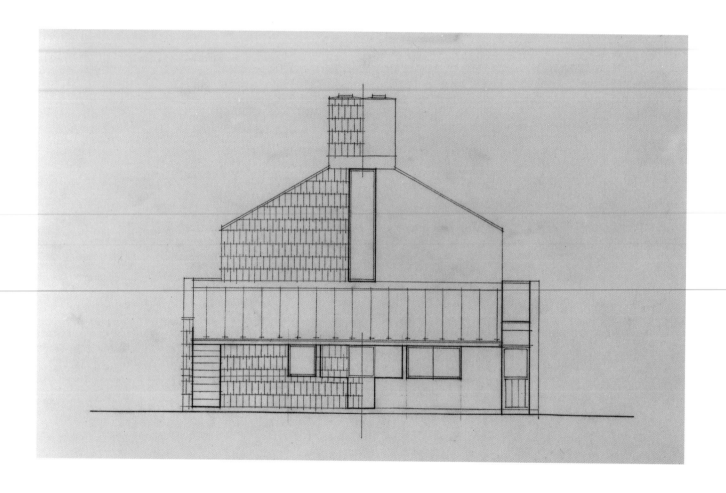

Front Elevation, east, pencil on vellum

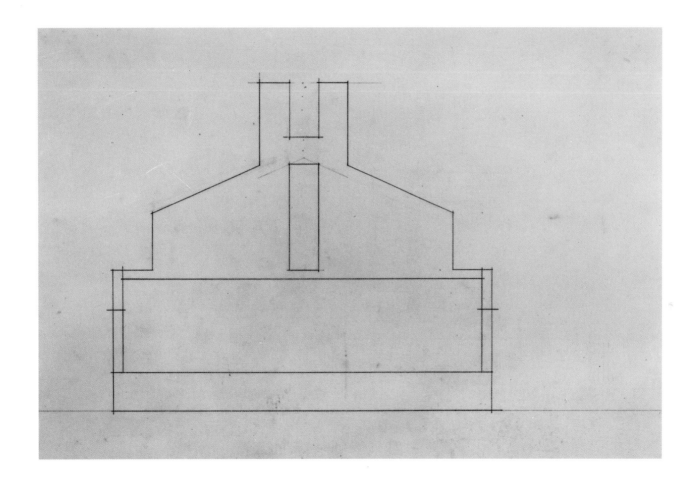

Rear Elevation, west, study, pencil on vellum

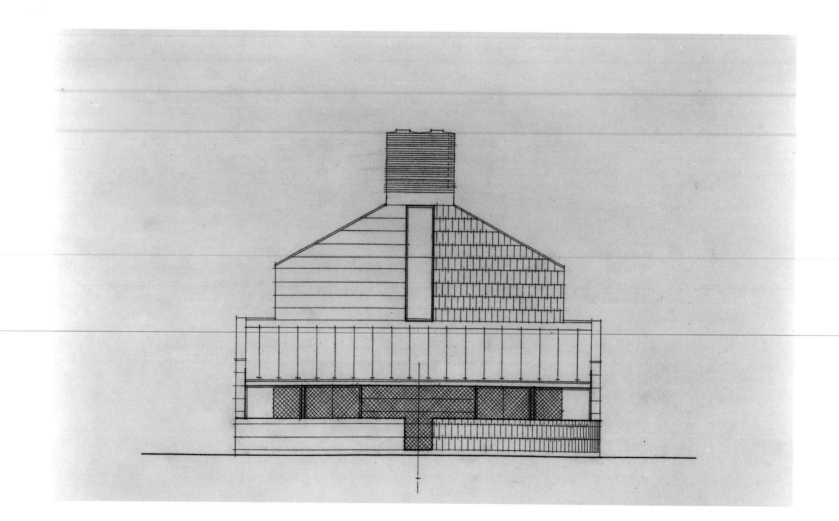

Rear Elevation, west, pencil on vellum

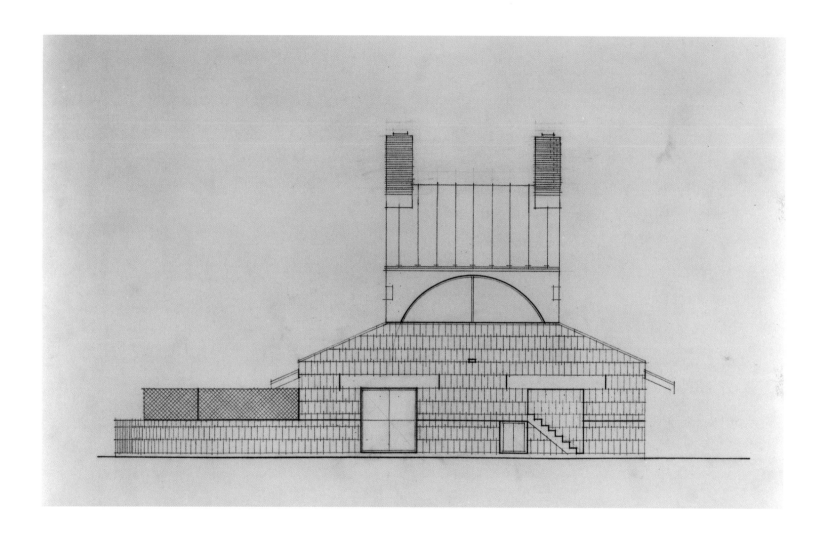

Side Elevation, south, pencil on vellum

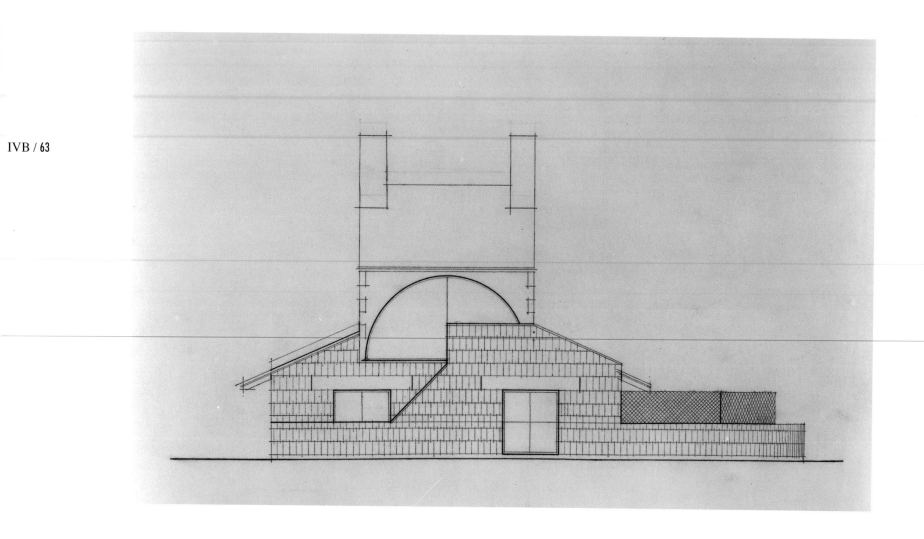

Side Elevation, north, pencil on vellum

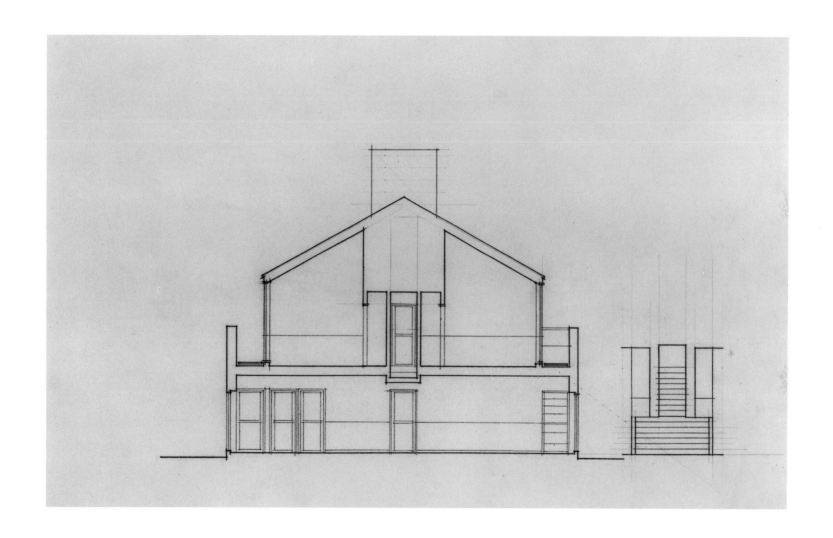

Section, pencil on vellum

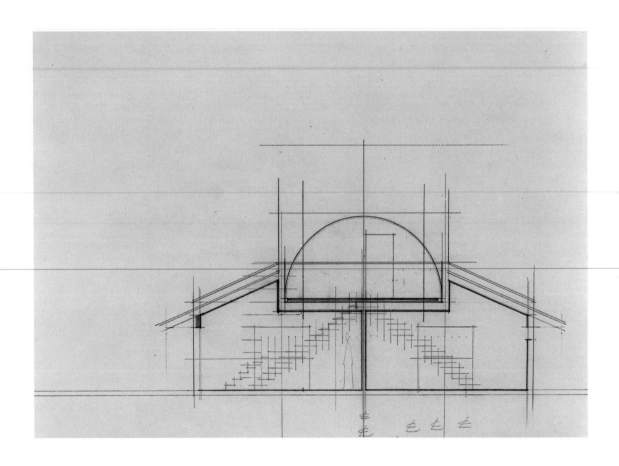

Section, study, pencil on vellum

Section, pencil on vellum

SCHEME

V

Model, chipboard and cut paper

145.

V

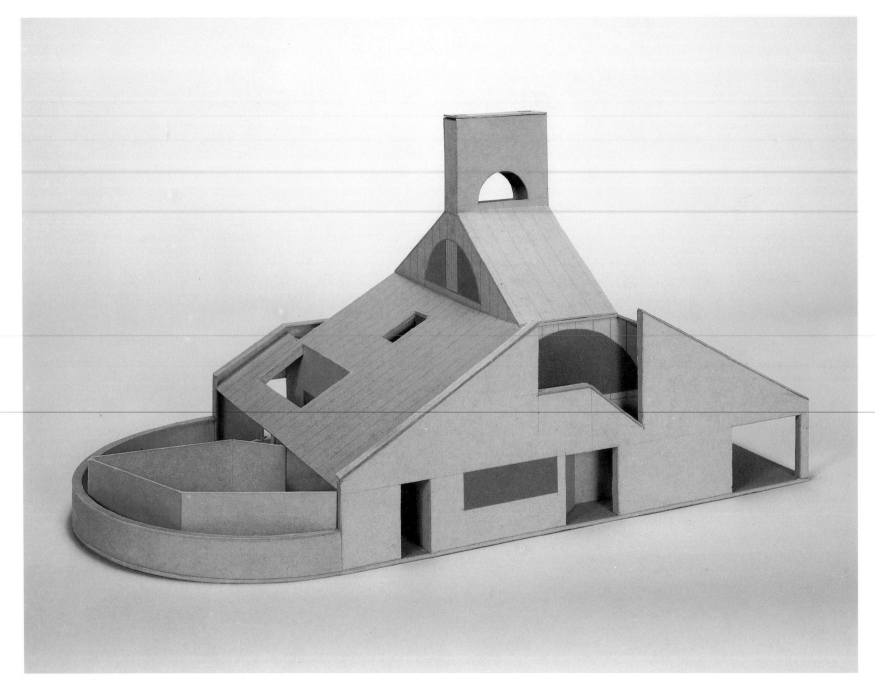

Model, chipboard and cut paper

146.

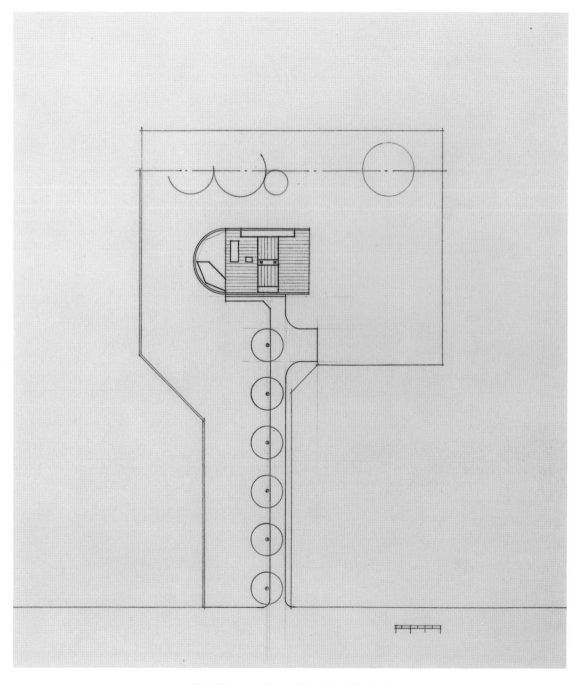

Plot Plan, pencil on vellum, June 12, 1962

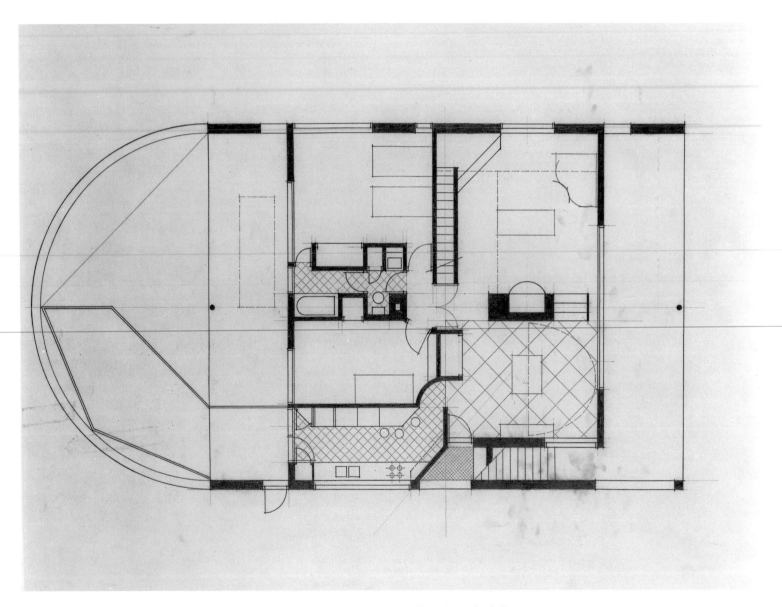

First Floor Plan, pencil on vellum, June 12, 1962

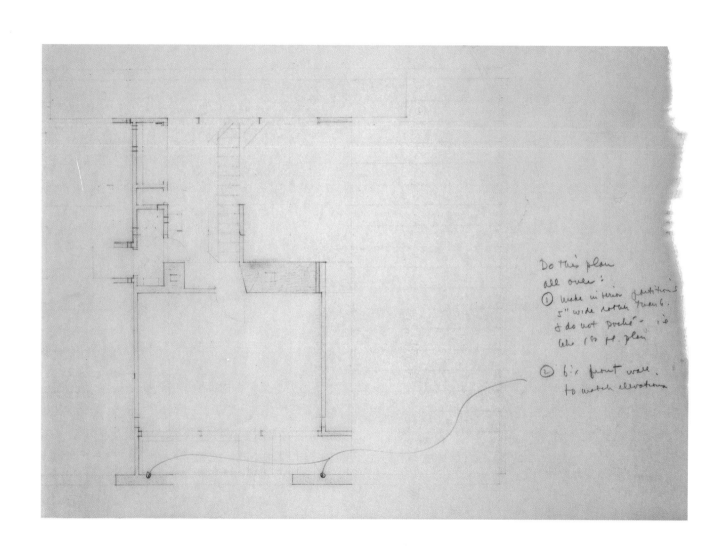

Second Floor Plan, study, pencil on cream trace

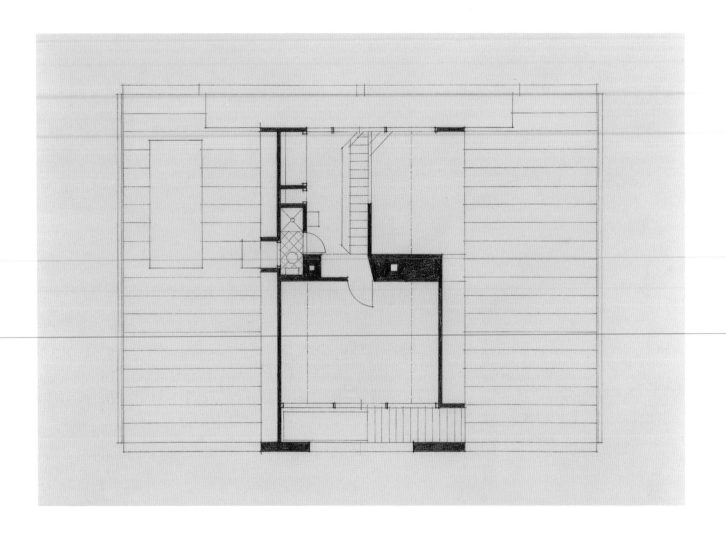

Second Floor Plan, pencil on vellum, June 12, 1962

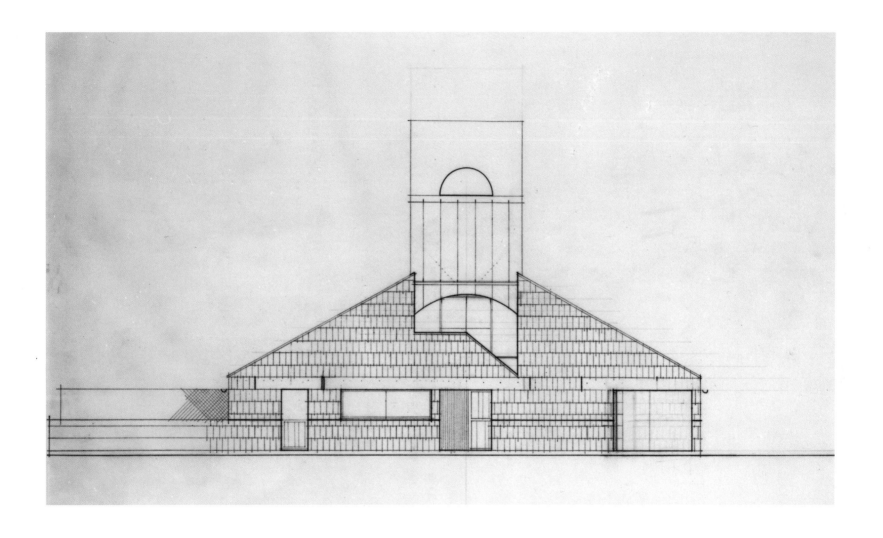

Front Elevation, east, pencil on vellum, June 12, 1962

Rear Elevation, west, pencil on vellum, June 12, 1962

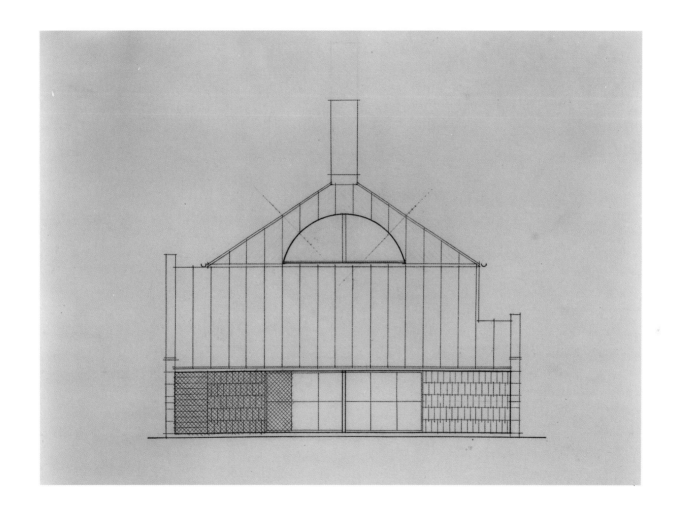

Side Elevation, north, pencil on vellum, June 12, 1962

Section, pencil on vellum, June 12, 1962

Section, pencil on vellum, June 12, 1962

SCHEME

VI

Model, chipboard and cut paper

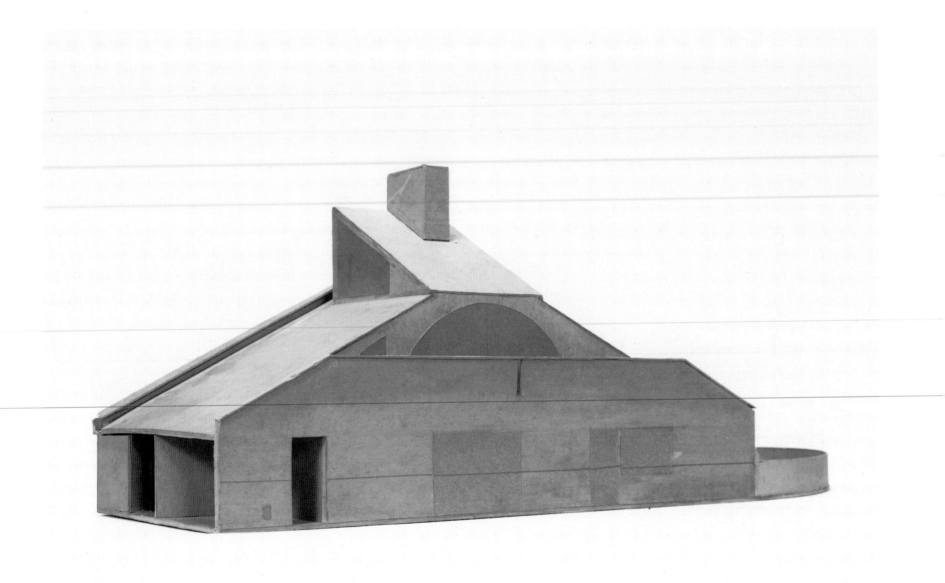

Model, chipboard and cut paper

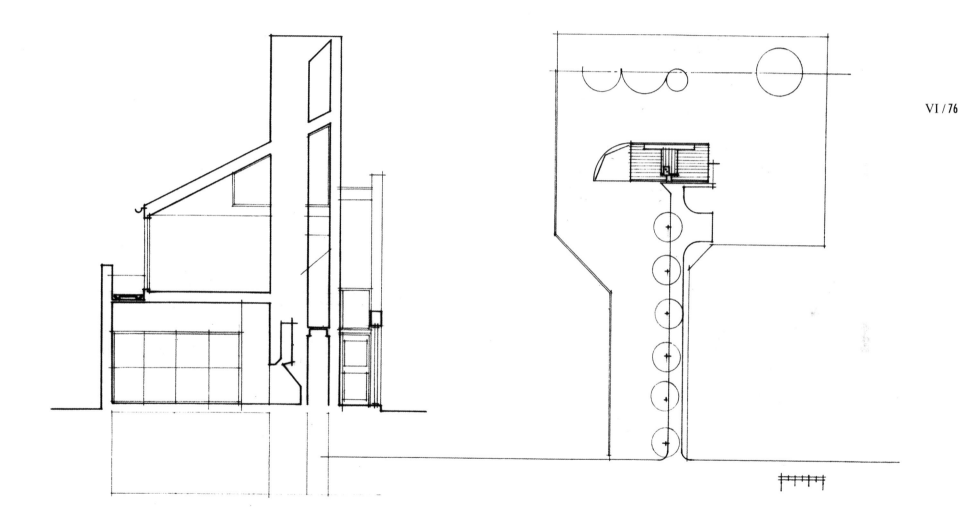

Plot Plan with Section, study, pencil on vellum, November 20, 1962

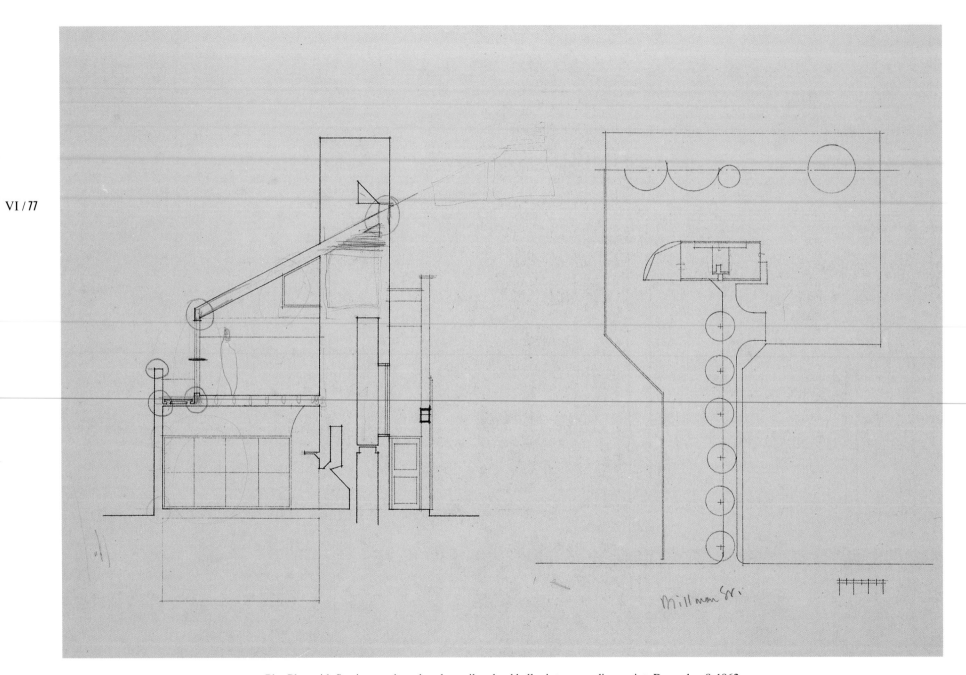

Plot Plan with Section, study, colored pencil and red ballpoint pen on diazo print, December 8, 1962

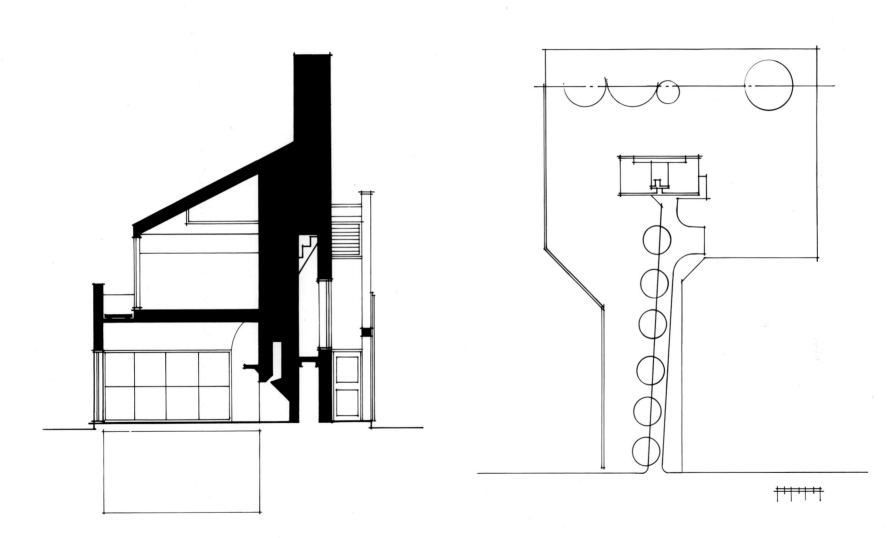

Plot Plan with Section, final presentation drawing, ink on mylar, December 8, 1962

First Floor Plan, study, pencil and colored pencil on vellum

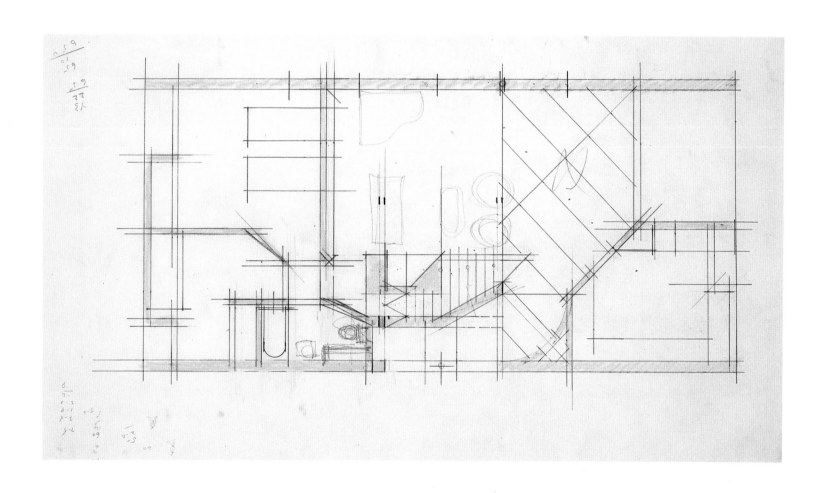

First Floor Plan, study, pencil and colored pencil on vellum

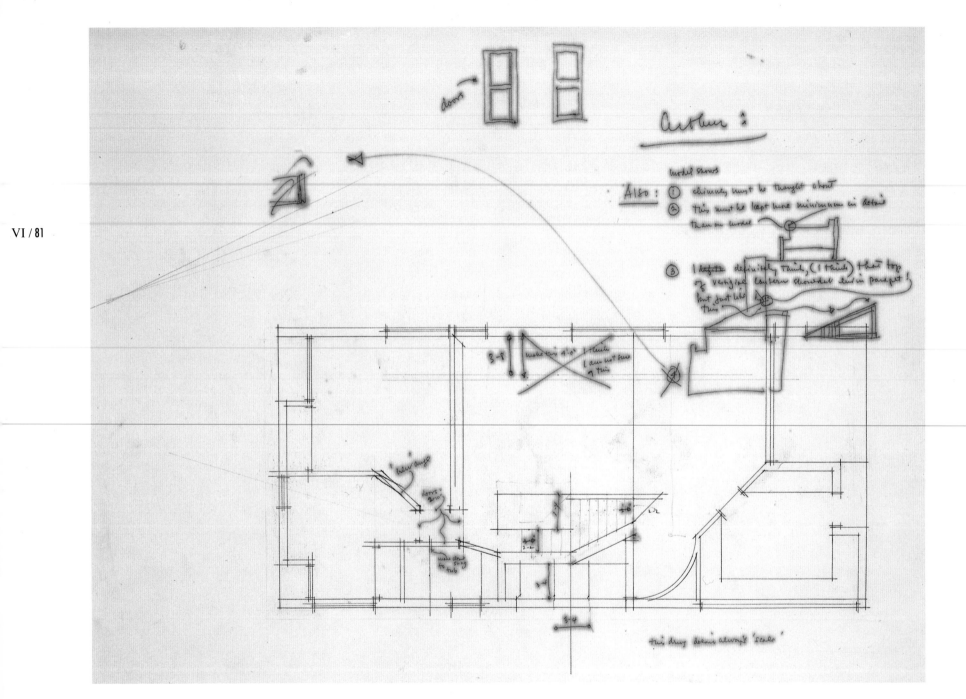

First Floor Plan, study, pencil and red ballpoint pen on vellum

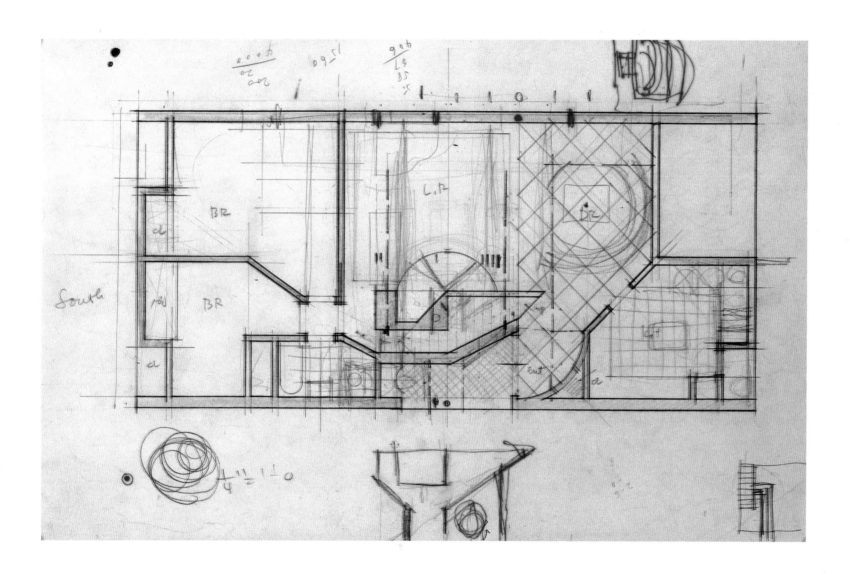

First Floor Plan, study, pencil, colored pencil and red ballpoint pen on vellum

VI / 83

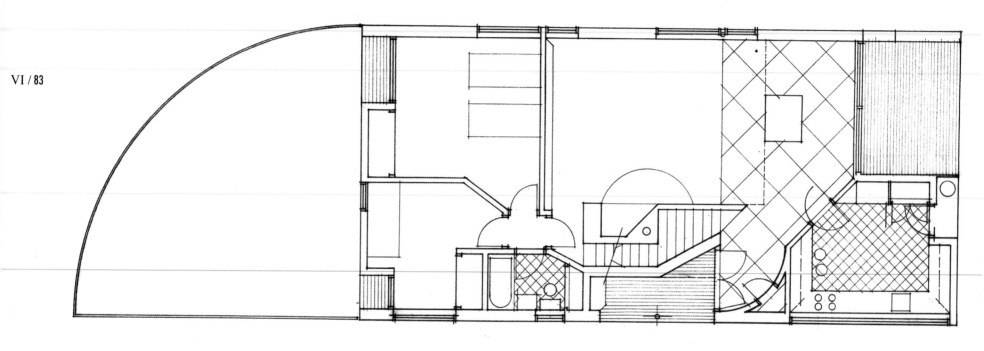

First Floor Plan, study, pencil on vellum

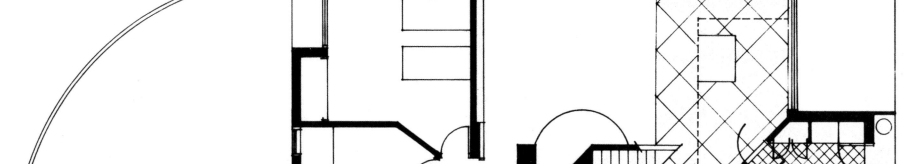

First Floor Plan, final presentation drawing, ink on mylar, December 8, 1962

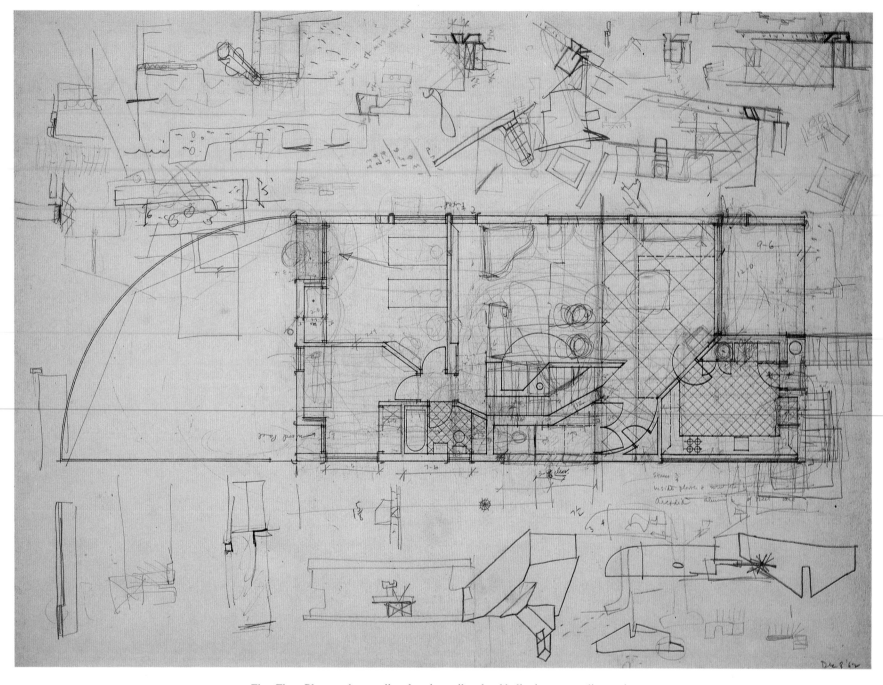

First Floor Plan, study, pencil, colored pencil and red ballpoint pen on diazo print

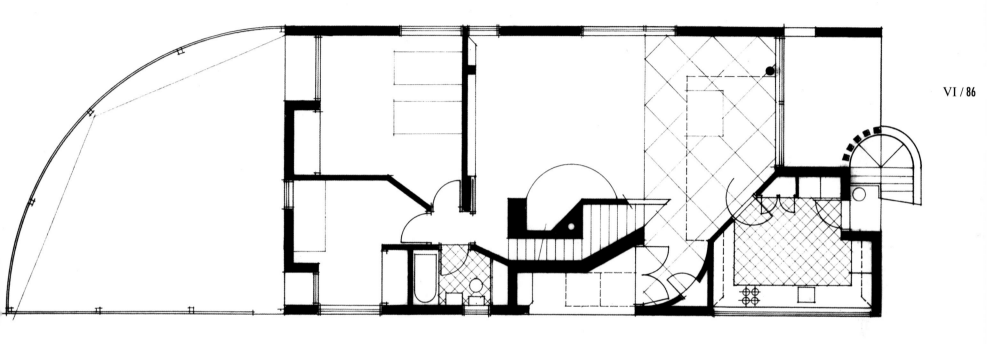

First Floor Plan, final presentation drawing, pencil on vellum, December 8, 1962

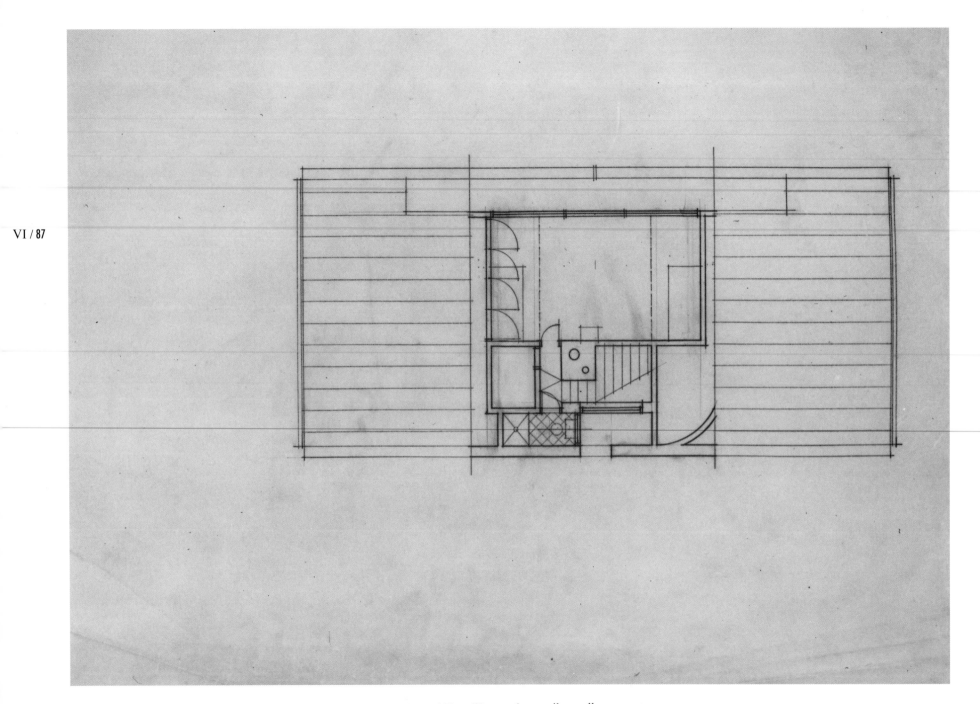

Second Floor Plan, study, pencil on vellum

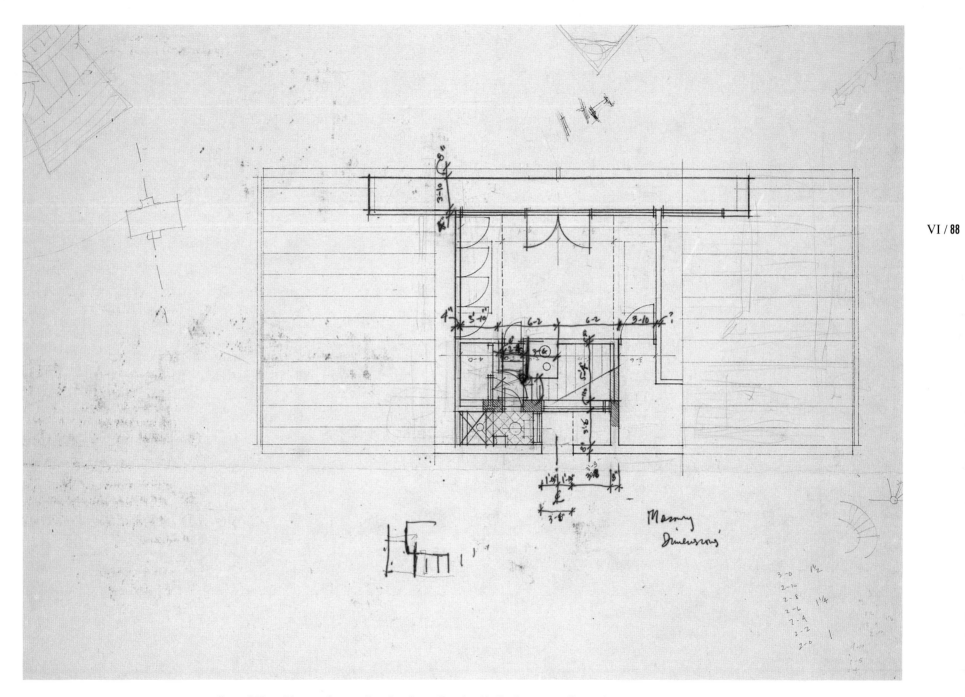

Second Floor Plan, study, pencil, colored pencil and red ballpoint pen on diazo print, December 8, 1962

Second Floor Plan, final presentation drawing, pencil on vellum, December 8, 1962

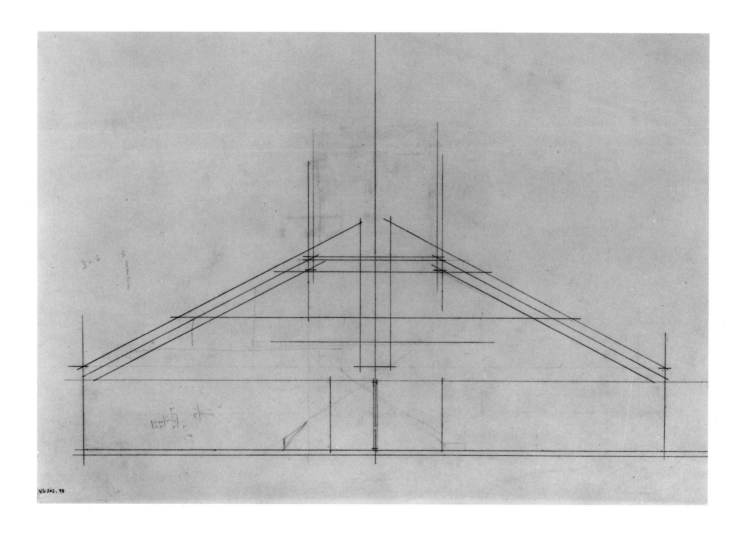

Front Elevation, east, study, pencil on vellum

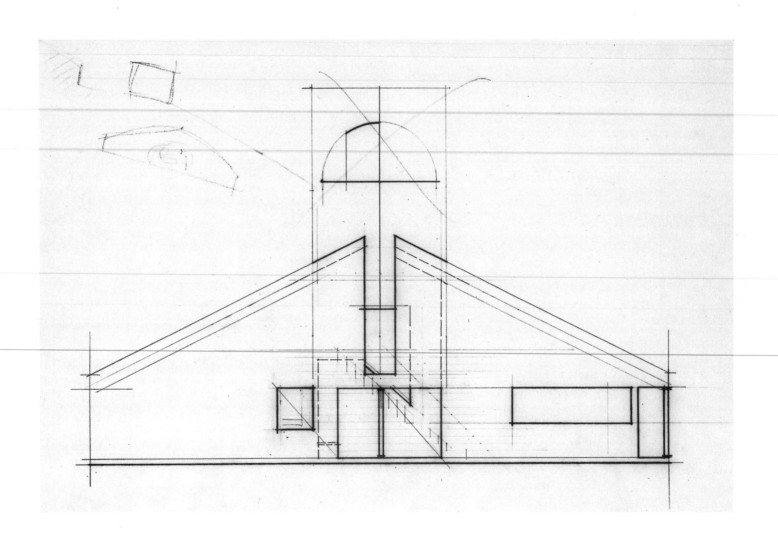

Front Elevation, east, study, pencil and colored pencil on vellum

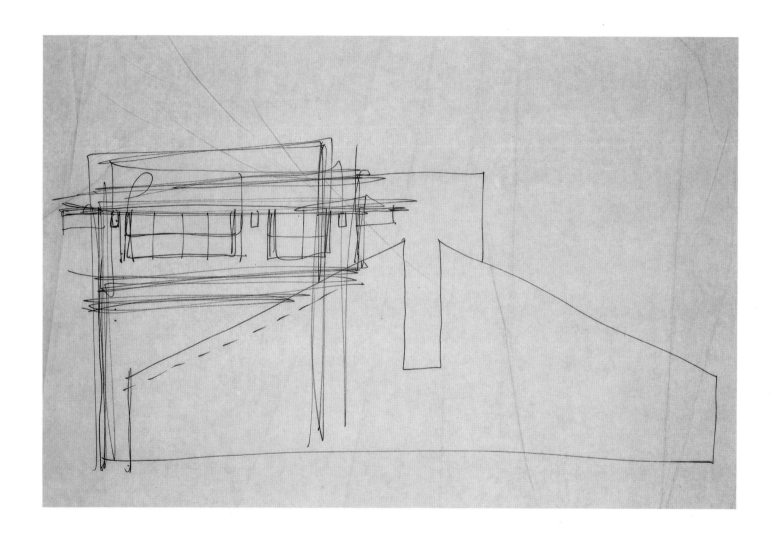

Front Elevation, east, study, black felt tip marker on yellow trace

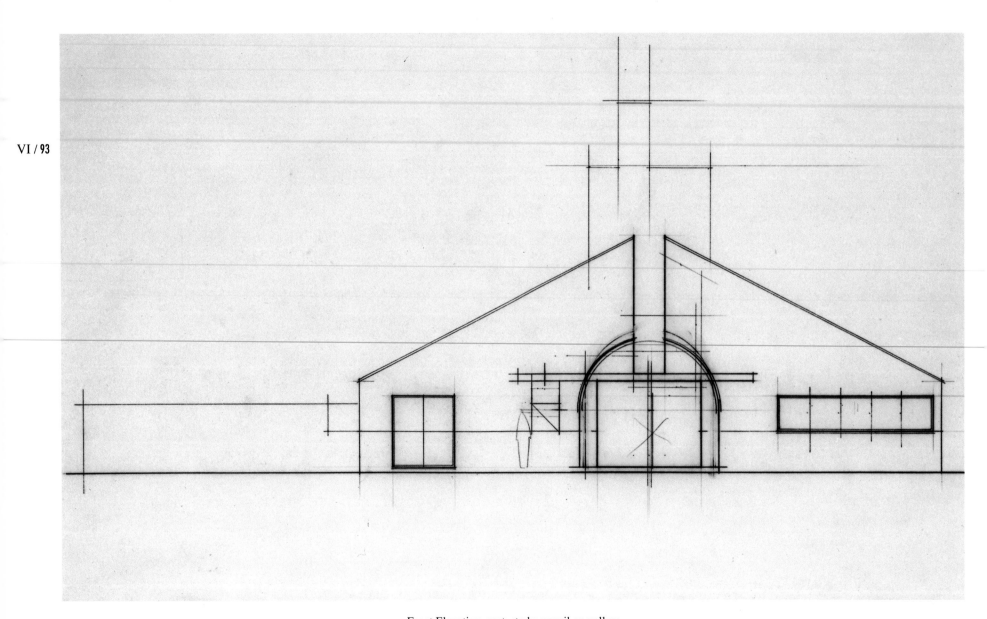

Front Elevation, east, study, pencil on vellum

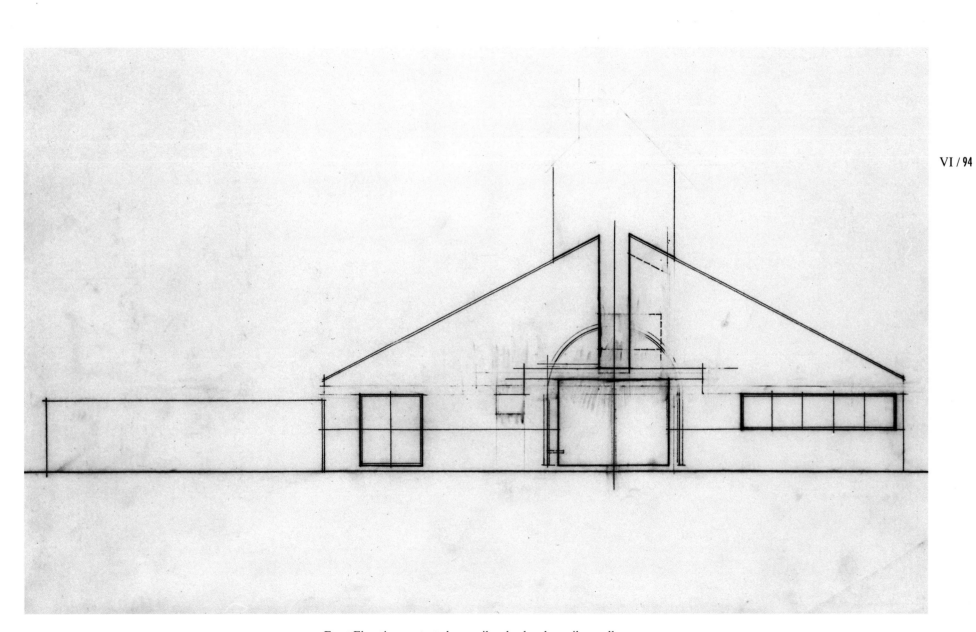

Front Elevation, east, study, pencil and colored pencil on vellum

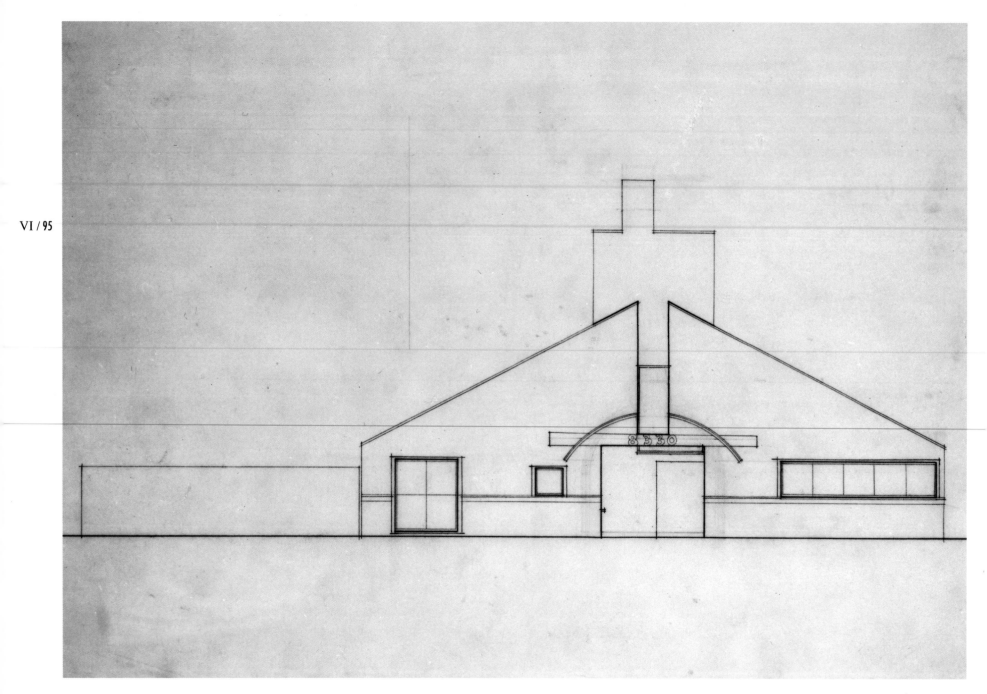

Front Elevation, east, presentation drawing, pencil on vellum, December 8, 1962

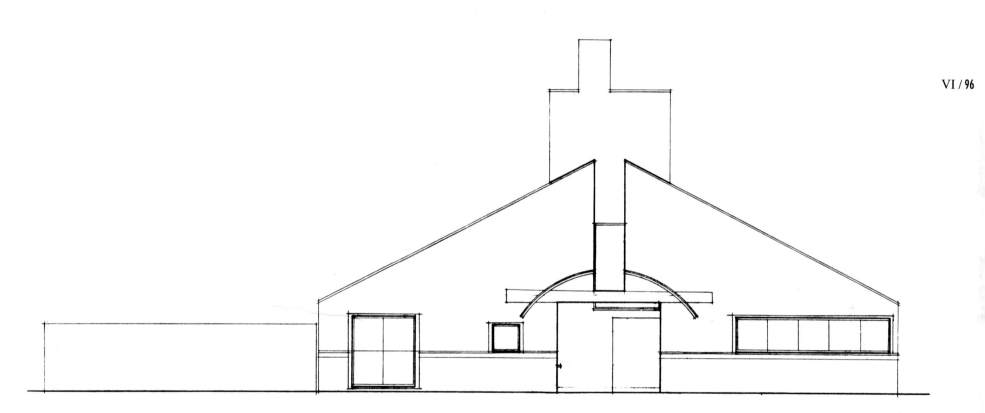

Front Elevation, east, final presentation drawing, ink on mylar, December 8, 1962

Rear Elevation, west, study, pencil on vellum

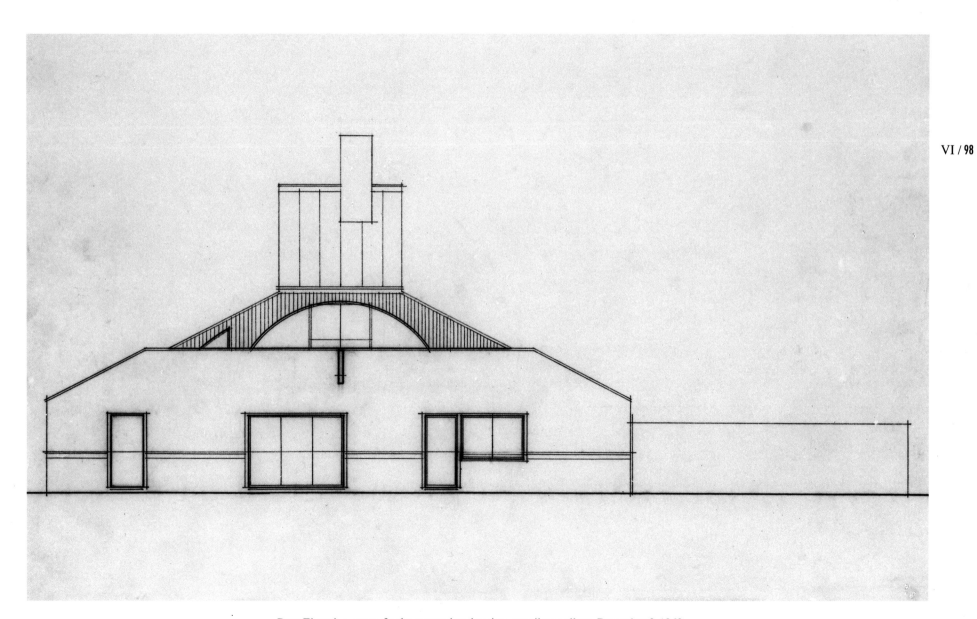

Rear Elevation, west, final presentation drawing, pencil on vellum, December 8, 1962

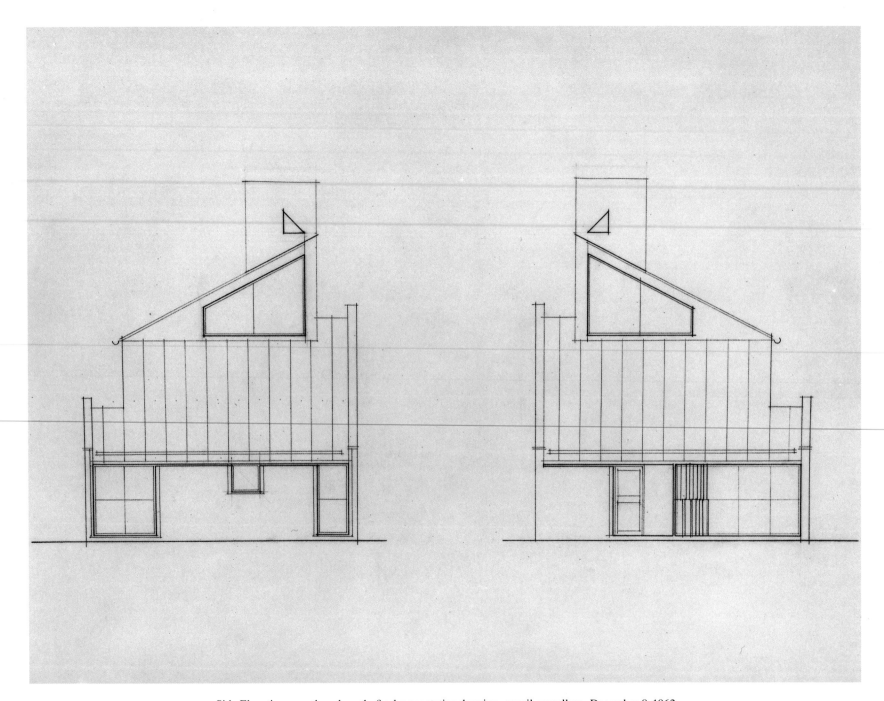

Side Elevations, north and south, final presentation drawing, pencil on vellum, December 8, 1962

Section, study, pencil on vellum, December 8, 1962

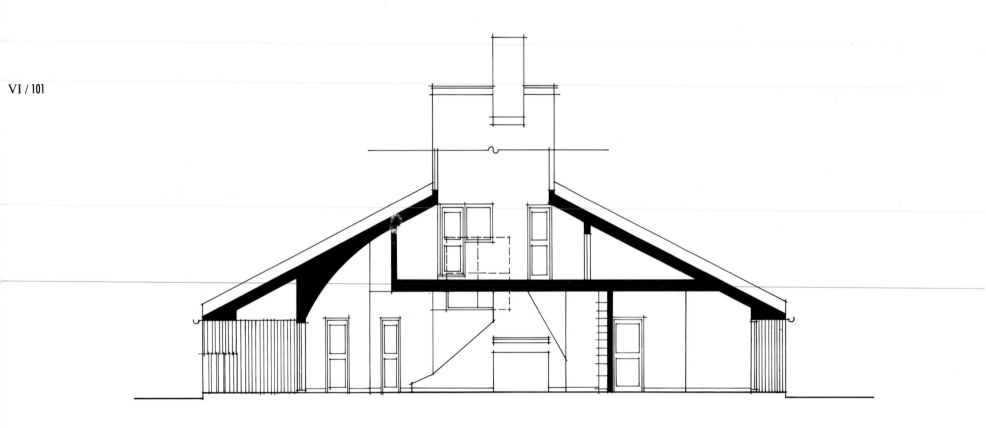

Section, final presentation drawing, ink on mylar

Section, study, pencil and red ballpoint pen on diazo print

CONSTRUCTION DRAWINGS

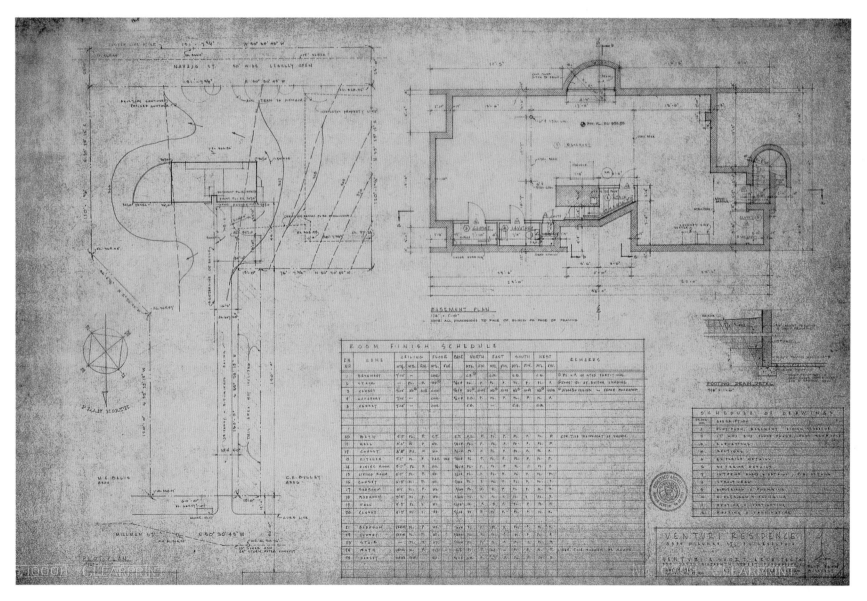

Plot Plan, Basement, Finish Schedule, sepia print of pencil on vellum, May 27, 1963

First and Second Floor Plans, Door Schedules, sepia print of pencil on vellum, May 24, 1963

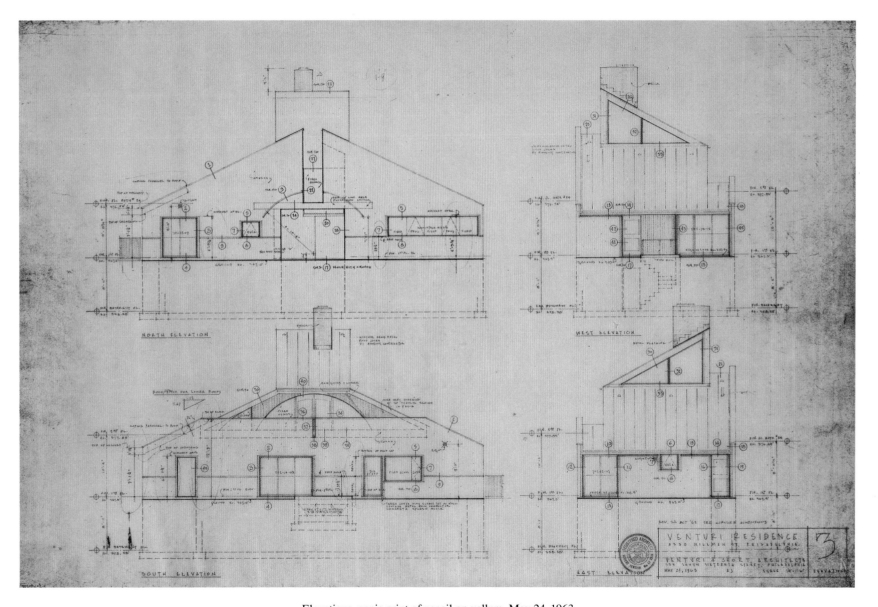

Elevations, sepia print of pencil on vellum, May 24, 1963

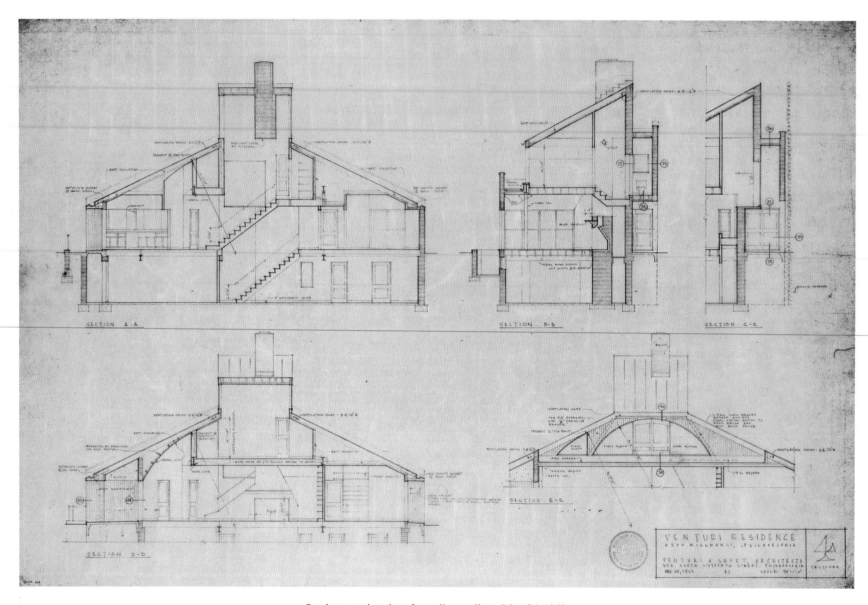

Sections, sepia print of pencil on vellum, May 24, 1963

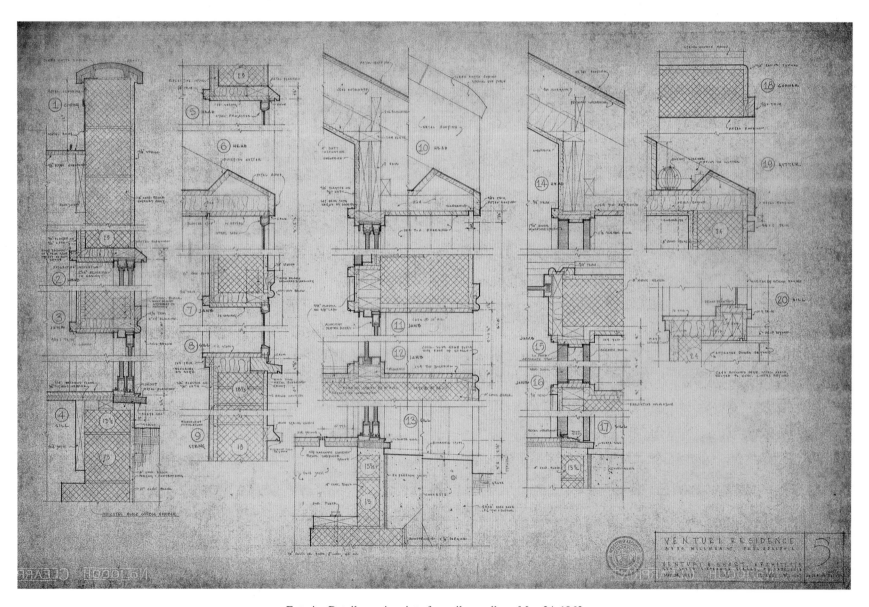

Exterior Details, sepia print of pencil on vellum, May 24, 1963

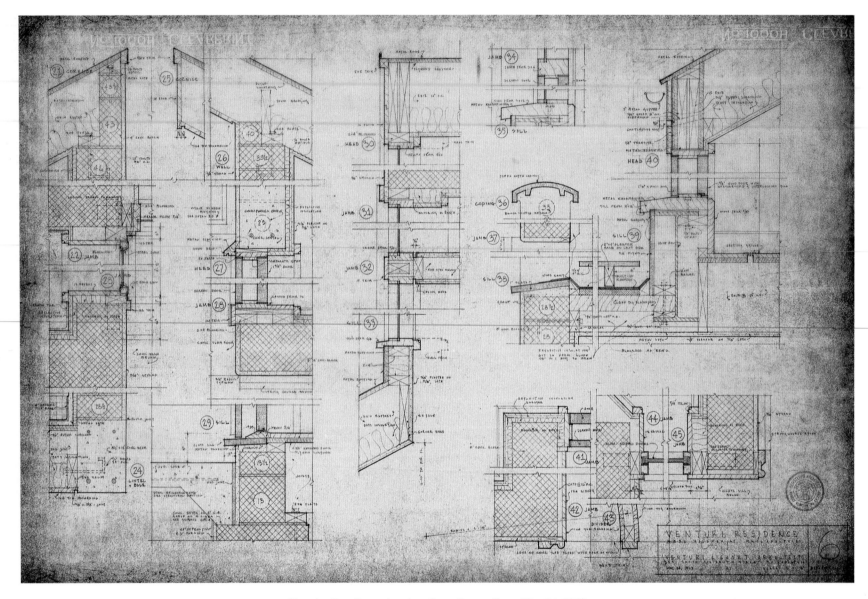

Exterior Details, sepia print of pencil on vellum, May 24, 1963

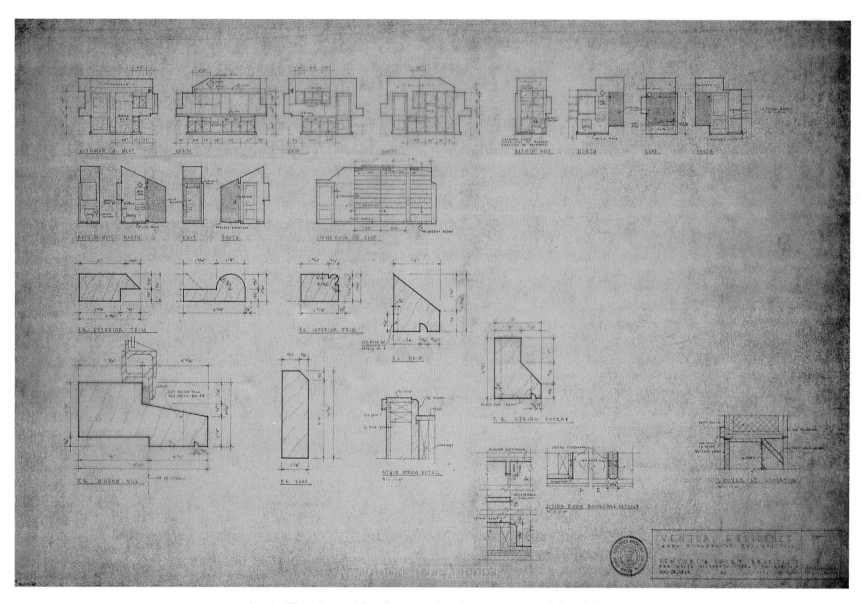

Interior Elevations and Details, sepia print of pencil on vellum, May 24, 1963

Structural Plans, sepia print of pencil on vellum, May 24, 1963

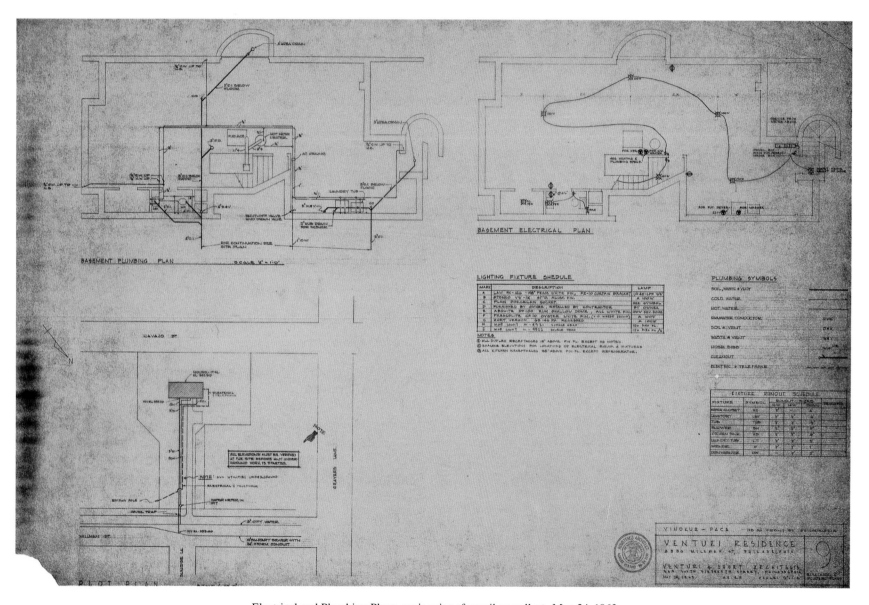

Electrical and Plumbing Plans, sepia print of pencil on vellum, May 24, 1963

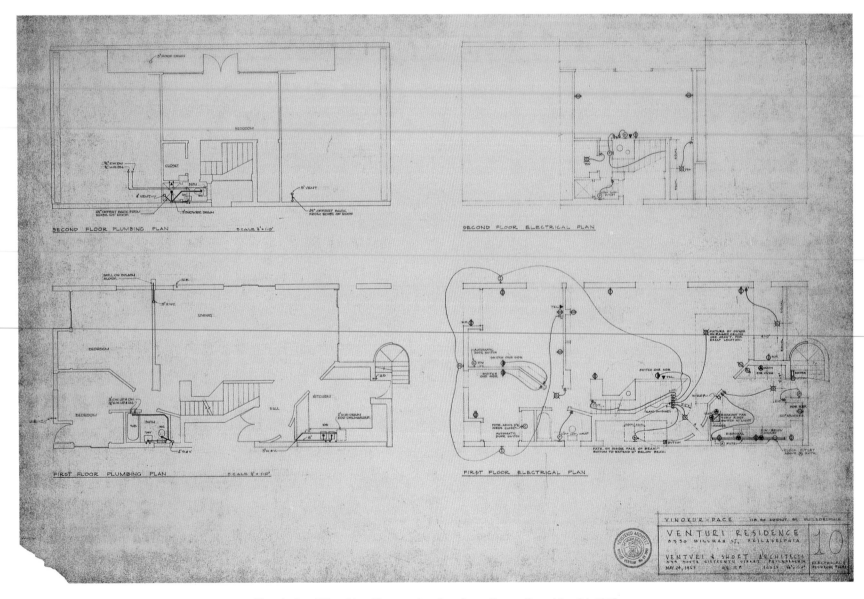

Electrical and Plumbing Plans, sepia print of pencil on vellum, May 24, 1963

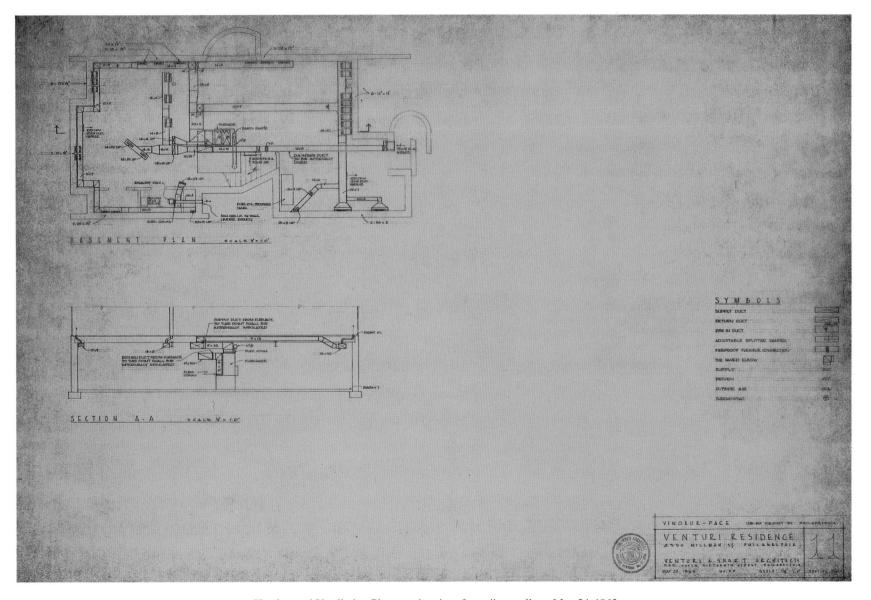

Heating and Ventilation Plans, sepia print of pencil on vellum, May 24, 1963

Heating and Ventilation Plans, sepia print of pencil on vellum, May 24, 1963

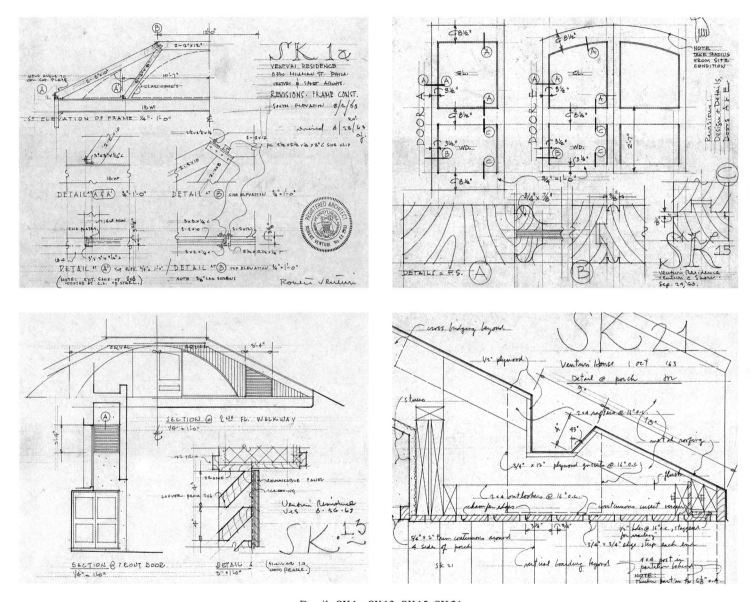

Details SK 1a, SK 13, SK 15, SK 21

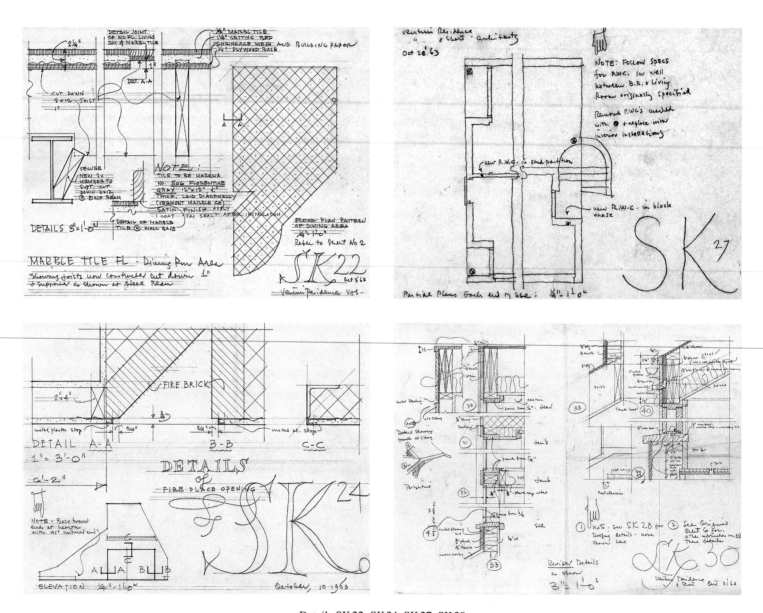

Details SK 22, SK 24, SK 27, SK 30

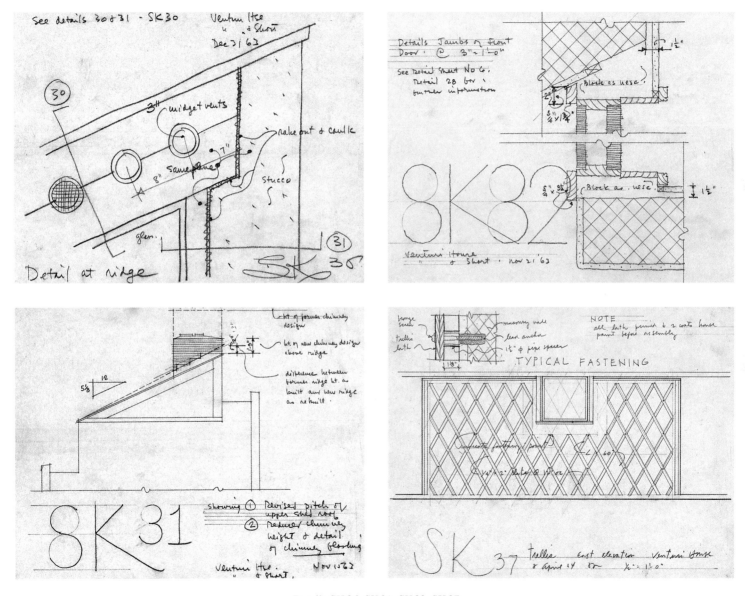

Details SK 36, SK 31, SK 32, SK 37

PHOTOGRAPHS

203.

212.

217.

BIOGRAPHY

Robert Venturi is one of the world's most important architects and theorists. Educated at Princeton University, he has taught at the University of Pennsylvania and Yale University, was the Architect in Residence at the American Academy in Rome, and has lectured widely in Europe and America. He has been the recipient of many design awards, including the Pritzker Architecture Prize, the Arnold W. Brunner Memorial Prize in Architecture, and the Hazlett Memorial Award for Excellence in the Arts. His book *Complexity and Contradiction in Architecture*, published in 1966, has been acknowledged as the most important writing on architecture since Le Corbusier's. Robert Venturi and Denise Scott Brown are partners in the firm Venturi, Scott Brown and Associates. Their recently completed buildings include the Seattle Art Museum and the Sainsbury Wing of the National Gallery in London.

BIBLIOGRAPHY

Architecture and the Arts Awards 1965,
"Vanna Venturi House," Architectural
League of New York, exhibition catalogue

"Complexities and Contradictions," *Progressive
Architecture*, May 1965, pp. 168–173

Crosbie, Michael, "Venturi's House for
his Mother Wins AIA 25-Year Award,"
Architecture, May 1989, p. 28

"Custom Houses by Young Architects,"
American Builder, October 1966,
pp. 60–61

"Five on Five," *Architectural Forum*,
May 1973, pp. 46–57

Goldberger, Paul, "Venturi and Rauch: Houses,"
Global Architecture, *Venturi and Rauch*,
GA 39, A.D.A. Edita, Tokyo, 1976, pp. 9–17

"Interview: Robert Venturi and Peter Eisenman,"
Skyline, July 1982, pp. 12–15

"Interview with Robert Venturi and Denise Scott
Brown," *Harvard Architecture Review*,
Volume 1, Spring 1980, pp. 228–239

Jencks, Charles, *The Language of Post-Modern
Architecture*, Rizzoli, New York, 1977

Klotz, Heinrich, *Postmodern Visions*,
Abbeville Press, New York, New York,
1985, pp. 325–330

Leigh, Catesby, "Visions of Venturi,"
Princeton Alumni Weekly, November 6,

1991, pp. 10–16

Lippard, Lucy R., *Pop Art*, Praeger,
New York, 1966

Osborne, Michelle, "A Personal Kind of
House," *Philadelphia Evening Bulletin*,
October 15, 1965, p. 55

"Pennsylvania Clinic," *The Architectural
Forum*, October 1963, p. 17

Schwartz, Frederic, and Vaccaro, Carolina,
Venturi, Scott Brown e Associati,
Zanichelli Editore, Bologna, 1991

Scott Brown, Denise, "A Worm's Eye View
of Recent Architectural History,"
Architectural Record, February 1984,
pp. 69–81

Scott Brown, Denise, and Venturi, Robert,
*A View from the Campidoglio, Selected
Essays 1953–1984*, edited by P. Arnell,
T. Bickford, and C. Begart, Harper & Row,
New York, 1984

Scott Brown, Denise, Venturi, Robert, and
Izenour, Steven, *Learning from Las Vegas*,
MIT Press, Cambridge, Massachusetts,
1972

Scully, Vincent, *The Shingle Style and The
Stick Style*, Yale University Press, New
Haven, 1955, revised edition, 1971

Stern, Robert A.M., *40 under 40*, Architectural

League of New York, 1966, catalogue
The Architecture of Robert Venturi,
University of New Mexico Press, 1989

Trumo, James Van, "The House Made with
Hands: Recent Houses Designed by
Philadelphia Architects," *Pennsylvania
Journal of Architecture*, November 1965,
pp. 10–15

"Venturi, Rauch and Scott Brown:
A Generation of Architecture," organized
by the Krannert Art Museum, University of
Illinois at Urbana-Champaign, exhibition
catalogue, 1984–86

Venturi, Robert, *Complexity and Contradiction
in Architecture*, with an introduction by
Vincent Scully, The Museum of Modern Art
Papers on Architecture, The Museum of
Modern Art, in association with the Graham
Foundation for the Advanced Studies in
the Fine Arts, 1966

Venturi, Robert, "Diversity, Relevance and
Representation in Historicism,
or Plus ça Change . . . plus A Plea
for Pattern all over Architecture with
a Postcript on my Mother's House."
The Walter Gropius Lecture, Graduate
School of Design, Harvard University, April
15, 1982, *Architectural Record*,

June 1982, pp. 114–119

Venturi, Robert, "Donald Drew Egbert—
A Tribute," *The Beaux-Arts Tradition in
French Architecture*, Princeton University
Press, 1980, pp. xiii–xiv

Venturi, Robert, "Response at the Pritzker Prize
Award Ceremony" at the Palacio de
Iturbide, Mexico City, Mexico, May 16,
1991, catalogue

Venturi, Robert, "Upbringing Among
Quakers," *Growing Up Italian*, by Lida
Brandi Cateura, William Morrow and
Company, New York, 1987, pp. 195–201

Venturi, Robert, and Scott Brown, Denise,
"Some Houses of Ill-Repute," *Perspecta
13/14*, Wittenborn and Company,
New York, 1969, pp. 258–267

Von Moos, Stanislaus, *Venturi, Rauch and
Scott Brown, Buildings and Projects*,
Rizzoli, New York, 1987

Wolfe, Tom, *From Bauhaus to Our House*,
Farrar Straus Giroux, New York,
New York, 1981

Wrede, Stuart, "Complexity and Contradiction
Twenty-five Years Later: An Interview
with Robert Venturi," *American Art of
the 1960s*, The Museum of Modern Art,
New York, 1991, pp. 143–163

DRAWING LIST

SCHEME I

1 Plot Plan
   pencil on vellum, 24 x 14 in., July 1959
   [v6202.12]
2 First Floor Plan
   pencil and colored pencil on yellow trace
   21.5 x 23.5 in., July 1959
   [v6202.11]
3 Rear Elevation, west
   pencil on vellum, 22 x 30 in., July 1959
   [v6202.9]
4 Side Elevation, south (with screen wall)
   pencil on vellum, 24.5 x 30.25 in.
   July 1959
   [v6202.17]
5 Side Elevation, south (without screen wall)
   pencil on vellum, 24.5 x 30.25 in.
   July 1959
   [v6202.16]
6 Section
   pencil on vellum, 22 x 30 in., July 1959
   [v6202.10]
7 Section
   pencil on vellum, 23 x 30 in., July 1959
   [v6202.18]

SCHEME IIA

8 First Floor Plan
   pencil on vellum, 24.5 x 30.25 in.
   July 19, 1959
   [v6202.30]
9 Framing Plan
   pencil on vellum, 24.5 x 30.25 in.
   July 19, 1959
   [v6202.32]
10 Front Elevation, east
   pencil on vellum, 24.5 x 30.25 in.
   July 19, 1959
   [v6202.13]
11 Rear Elevation, west
   pencil on vellum, 24.5 x 30.25 in.
   July 19, 1959
   [v6202.14]
12 Side Elevation, south (with screen wall)
   pencil on vellum, 24.5 x 30.25 in.
   July 19, 1959
   [v6202.19]
13 Section
   pencil on vellum, 24.5 x 30.25 in.
   July 19, 1959
   [v6202.15]

14 Section
   pencil on vellum, 24.5 x 30.25 in.
   July 19, 1959
   [v6202.20]

SCHEME IIB

15 Plot Plan
   pencil on vellum, 30 x 30 in.
   August 31, 1959
   [v6202.33]
16 First Floor Plan
   pencil on vellum, 30 x 30 in.
   August 31, 1959
   [v6202.34]
17 Rear Elevation, west
   pencil on vellum, 30 x 30 in.
   August 31, 1959
   [v6202.39]
18 Side Elevation, south (with screen wall)
   pencil on vellum, 30 x 30 in.
   August 31, 1959
   [v6202.38]
19 Perspective from southwest
   pencil on vellum, 30 x 30 in.
   August 31, 1959
   [v6202.40]

20 Section
   pencil on vellum, 30 x 30 in.
   August 31, 1959
   [v6202.37]
21 Section
   pencil on vellum, 30 x 30 in.
   August 31, 1959
   [v6202.36]

SCHEME IIC

22 Plot Plan
   pencil on vellum, 24 x 24 in.
   [v6202.26]
23 Roof Framing Plan
   pencil on vellum, 24 x 24 in.
   [v6202.31]
24 Roof Plan
   pencil on vellum, 24 x 24 in.
   [v6202.28]
25 Front Elevation, east
   pencil on vellum, 24 x 24 in.
   [v6202.23]
26 Rear Elevation, west
   pencil on vellum, 24 x 24 in.
   [v6202.24]

27 Side Elevation, north, study
    pencil on vellum, 24 x 24 in.

28 Side Elevation, north
    pencil on vellum, 24 x 24 in.

29 Section
    pencil on vellum, 24 x 24 in.
    [v6202.25]

30 Section
    pencil on vellum, 24 x 24 in.
    [v6202.22]

SCHEME IIIA

31 Plot Plan
    pencil on vellum, 18 x 22.5 in.
    [v6202.41]

32 First Floor Plan
    pencil on vellum, 18 x 22.5 in.
    [v6202.42]

33 Front Elevation, east
    pencil on vellum, 18 x 22.5 in.
    [v6202.54]

34 Front Elevation, east
    pencil on vellum, 18 x 22.5 in.
    [v6202.52]

35 Side Elevation, south
    pencil on vellum, 18 x 22.5 in.
    [DAM 83/851]

36 Front Elevation, north
    pencil on vellum, 18 x 22.5 in.
    [v6202.50]

37 Section
    pencil on vellum, 18 x 22.5 in.
    [v6202.48]

38 Section
    pencil on vellum, 18 x 22.5 in.
    [v6202.46]

SCHEME IIIB

39 First Floor Plan
    pencil on vellum, 18 x 22.5 in.
    [v6202.43]

40 Front Elevation, east
    pencil on vellum, 18 x 22.5 in.
    [v6202.53]

41 Rear Elevation, west
    pencil on vellum, 18 x 22.5 in.
    [v6202.51]

42 Side Elevation, south
    pencil on vellum, 18 x 22.5 in.
    [v6202.49]

43 Side Elevation, north
    pencil on vellum, 18 x 22.5 in.
    [vrsb 25]

44 Section
    pencil on vellum, 18 x 22.5 in.
    [v6202.45]

SCHEME IVA

45 Plot Plan
    pencil on vellum, 18 x 24 in., July 12, 1961
    [v6202.79]

46 First Floor Plan
    pencil on vellum, 18 x 24 in., July 12, 1961
    [v6202.80]

47 Second Floor Plan
    pencil on vellum, 18 x 24 in., July 12, 1961
    [v6202.81]

48 Front Elevation, east
    pencil on vellum, 18 x 24 in., July 12, 1961
    [v6202.84]

49 Side Elevation, south, study
    pencil on vellum, 14.5 x 19.5 in.
    [v6202.65]

50 Side Elevation, south
    pencil on vellum, 18 x 24 in., July 12, 1961
    [v6202.85]

51 Side Elevation, north
    pencil on vellum, 18 x 24 in., July 12, 1961
    [v6202.86]

52 Section
    pencil on vellum, 18 x 24 in., July 12, 1961
    [v6202.82]

53 Section
    pencil on vellum, 18 x 24 in., July 12, 1961
    [v6202.83]

SCHEME IVB

54 Plot Plan
    pencil on vellum, 18 x 24 in.
    [v6202.55]

55 First Floor Plan, study
    pencil on vellum, 18 x 24 in.
    [v6202.57]

56 First Floor Plan
    pencil on vellum, 18 x 24 in.
    [v6202.56]

57 Second Floor Plan
    pencil on vellum, 18 x 24 in.
    [v6202.58]

58 Front Elevation, east, study
    pencil on vellum, 18 x 16.5 in.
    [v6202.87]

59 Front Elevation, east
    pencil on vellum, 18 x 24 in.
    [v6202.67]

60 Rear Elevation, west, study
    pencil on vellum, 18 x 24 in.
    [v6202.88]

61 Rear Elevation, west
    pencil on vellum, 18 x 24 in.
    [v6202.68]

62 Side Elevation, south
    pencil on vellum, 18 x 24 in.
    [v6202.64]

63 Side Elevation, north
    pencil on vellum, 18 x 24 in.
    [v6202.66]

64 Section
    pencil on vellum, 18 x 24 in.
    [v6202.63]

65 Section, study
    pencil on vellum, 12 x 20.5 in.
    [v6202.60]

66 Section
    pencil on vellum, 18 x 24 in.
    [v6202.59]

SCHEME V

67 Plot Plan
    pencil on vellum, 18 x 24 in.
    June 12, 1962
    [v6202.69]

68 First Floor Plan
    pencil on vellum, 18 x 24 in.
    June 12, 1962
    [v6202.70]

69 Second Floor Plan, study
    pencil on cream trace, 12 x 16 in.
    [v6202.72]

70 Second Floor Plan
    pencil on vellum, 18 x 24 in.
    June 12, 1962
    [v6202.73]

71 Front Elevation, east
    pencil on vellum, 18 x 24 in.
    June 12, 1962
    [vrsb 254]

72 Rear Elevation, west
    pencil on vellum, 18 x 24 in.
    June 12, 1962
    [v6202.78]

73 Side Elevation, north
    pencil on vellum, 18 x 24 in.
    June 12, 1962
    [v6202.77]

74 Section
    pencil on vellum, 18 x 24 in.
    June 12, 1962
    [v6202.74]

75 Section
    pencil on vellum, 18 x 24 in.
    June 12, 1962
    [v6202.75]

SCHEME VI

76 Plot Plan with Section, study
  pencil on vellum, 18 x 24 in.
  November 20, 1962
  [DAM 83/857]

77 Plot Plan with Section, study
  colored pencil and red ballpoint pen
  on diazo print, 18 x 24.5 in.
  December 8, 1962
  [v6202.114]

78 Plot Plan with Section, final presentation
  drawing
  ink on mylar, 8 x 12 in.
  December 8, 1962
  [v6202.90]

79 First Floor Plan, study
  pencil and colored pencil on vellum
  18 x 24 in.
  [v6202.91]

80 First Floor Plan, study
  pencil and colored pencil on vellum
  12 x 18 in.
  [v6202.93]

81 First Floor Plan, study
  pencil and red ballpoint pen on vellum
  18 x 24 in.
  [v6202.94]

82 First Floor Plan, study
  pencil, colored pencil and red ballpoint
  pen on vellum, 18 x 24 in.
  [DAM 83/850]

83 First Floor Plan, study
  pencil on vellum, 18 x 24 in.
  [DAM 83/854]

84 First Floor Plan, final presentation drawing
  ink on mylar, 8 x 12 in.
  December 8, 1962

85 First Floor Plan, study
  pencil, colored pencil and red ballpoint
  pen on diazo print, 18 x 24.5 in.
  [v6202.115]

86 First Floor Plan, final presentation drawing
  pencil on vellum, 18 x 24 in.
  December 8, 1962
  [DAM 83/848]

87 Second Floor Plan, study
  pencil on vellum, 18 x 24 in.
  [v6202.95]

88 Second Floor Plan, study
  pencil, colored pencil and red ballpoint
  pen on diazo print, 18 x 24.5 in.
  December 8, 1962
  [v6202.116]

89 Second Floor Plan, final presentation
  drawing
  pencil on vellum, 18 x 24 in.
  December 8, 1962
  [v6202.96]

90 Front Elevation, east, study
  pencil on vellum, 12 x 18 in.
  [v6202.98]

91 Front Elevation, east, study
  pencil and colored pencil on vellum
  12 x 18 in.
  [DAM 83/899]

92 Front Elevation, east, study
  black felt tip marker on yellow trace
  18 x 22 in.
  [v6202.4]

93 Front Elevation, east, study
  pencil on vellum, 18 x 24 in.
  [DAM 83/85]

94 Front Elevation, east, study
  pencil and colored pencil on vellum
  18 x 24 in.
  [DAM 83/847]

95 Front Elevation, east, presentation drawing
  pencil on vellum, 18 x 24 in.
  December 8, 1962

96 Front Elevation, east, final presentation
  drawing
  ink on mylar, 8 x 12 in.
  December 8, 1962

97 Rear Elevation, west, study
  pencil on vellum, 18 x 24 in.
  [DAM 83/851]

98 Rear Elevation, west, final presentation
  drawing
  pencil on vellum, 18 x 24 in.
  December 8, 1962
  [DAM 83/852]

99 Side Elevations, north and south, final
  presentation drawing
  pencil on vellum, 18 x 24 in.
  December 8, 1962
  [v6202.99]

100 Section, study
  pencil on vellum, 18 x 24 in.
  December 8, 1962
  [v6202.97]

101 Section, final presentation drawing
  ink on mylar, 8 x 12 in.

102 Section, study
  pencil and red ballpoint pen on diazo print
  18 x 24 in.
  [v6202.117]

CONSTRUCTION DRAWINGS

103 Plot Plan, Basement, Finish Schedule
  sepia print of pencil on vellum, 24 x 36 in.
  May 27, 1963
  [v6202.101]

104 First and Second Floor Plans, Door
  Schedules
  sepia print of pencil on vellum, 24 x 36 in.
  May 24, 1963
  [v6202.102]

105 Elevations
  sepia print of pencil on vellum, 24 x 36 in.
  May 24, 1963
  [v6202.103]

106 Sections
  sepia print of pencil on vellum, 24 x 36 in.
  May 24, 1963
  [v6202.104]

107 Exterior Details
  sepia print of pencil on vellum, 24 x 36 in.
  May 24, 1963
  [v6202.105]

108 Exterior Details
  sepia print of pencil on vellum, 24 x 36 in.
  May 24, 1963
  [v6202.106]

109 Interior Elevations and Details
  sepia print of pencil on vellum, 24 x 36 in.
  May 24, 1963
  [v6202.107]

110 Structural Plans
  sepia print of pencil on vellum, 24 x 36 in.
  May 24, 1963
  [v6202.108]

111 Electrical and Plumbing Plans
  sepia print of pencil on vellum, 24 x 36 in.
  May 24, 1963
  [v6202.109]

112 Electrical and Plumbing Plans
  sepia print of pencil on vellum, 24 x 36 in.
  May 24, 1963
  [v6202.110]

113 Heating and Ventilation Plans
  sepia print of pencil on vellum, 24 x 36 in.
  May 24, 1963
  [v6202.111]

114 Heating and Ventilation Plans
  sepia print of pencil on vellum, 24 x 36 in.
  May 24, 1963
  [v6202.112]